W9-DGI-767

Story of
Australia

The Story of Australia - a Childcraft title
Childcraft Reg. U.S. Pat. & T.M. Off. Marca Registrada

1993 Revised Printing

World Book, Inc.
525 W. Monroe
Chicago, IL 60661
U.S.A.

Printed in the United States of America

ISBN: 0-7166-6453-4

F/IC

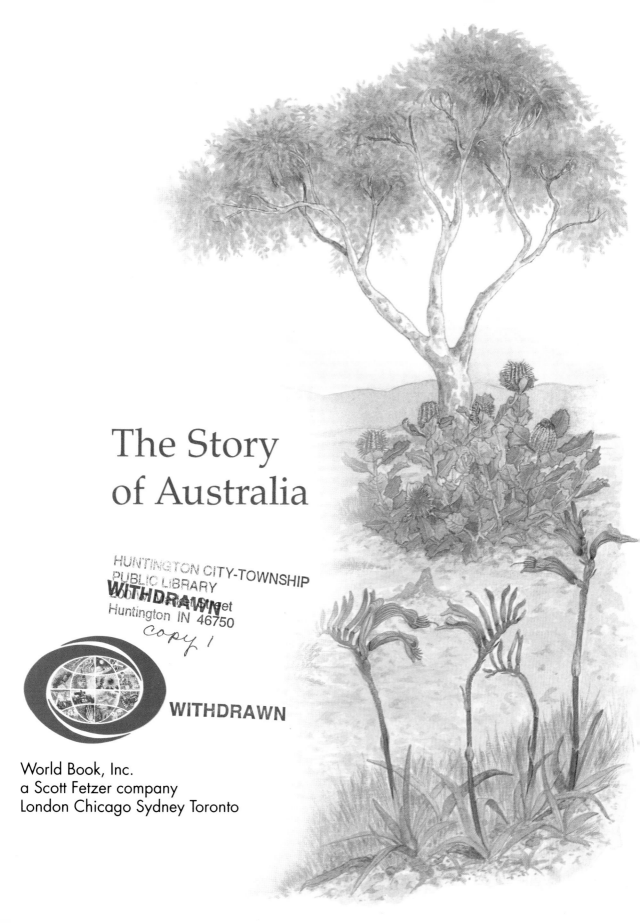

The Story
of Australia

World Book, Inc.
a Scott Fetzer company
London Chicago Sydney Toronto

Publishing Director: Felicia Law
Managing Editor: Pip Morgan
Project Editor: Gerry Bailey
Editor: Alice Webb
Author: Janine Amos
Designer: Frank Peglar
Picture Research: Samantha Bentham
Production Manager: Christine McKenzie

Consultants: Keith J. Solomon,
Assistant Vice-Chancellor,
Northern Territory University

Geoffrey Bolton,
Professor of Australian History,
Murdoch University

Rob Watkins,
Primary Teacher,
Granard Junior School,
London, UK

World Book would also like to thank the following for their help
and assistance:

John McQuilton Ph.D., Assistant General Editor 'Australia, 1788-
1988 — A Bicentennial History'

Professor R.M. Berndt, Dept. of Anthropology University of Western
Australia

Contents

In the beginning

In the beginning the world was waiting. Nothing moved and no sound was heard. But, deep in dark and icy caverns lay the Dreaming Spirits. They were not yet awake. They lay sleeping in the cold darkness, waiting for life.

At last they stirred and woke up! Then they began to move over the land. Many of the Dreaming Spirits looked like men and women.

But they were called by the names of plants, animals, birds, clouds or stars. They strode about, shaping the land like clay. They made the waters and the dry stretches, the billabongs

and the sandhills. They made the countryside comfortable for human beings.

This is an Aboriginal story, telling how the first Aborigines came to be in Australia. Many Aborigines say their people have lived there since the beginning of time. They believe they came from the Spirits of the Dreaming and are very proud of this.

In fact no one is sure exactly how long the Aborigines have been in Australia, or where they came from. Perhaps they came from South-East Asia when the sea levels were lower and the crossing easier than now. But we do know that the Aborigines have lived in Australia for well over 50,000 years.

Food from the land

The little girl followed her mother and aunt through the grass. She was out helping to gather the family's food, and the three of them had been up since dawn. The two women carried digging sticks and wooden bowls, and the little girl trotted behind. In her arms she held two baskets called dillybags which were made of plaited reeds.

When the first European explorers visited Australia, they thought that the Aborigines lived only on fish. But the Aborigines ate many other things — their food was just very different from that eaten by the Europeans.

Women and children gathered most of the family's food from the countryside around. Sometimes they looked for frogs, birds and birds' eggs, or small rats and mice which they dug out of holes in the ground with their hands or with sticks. They also searched for insects like witchetty grubs or the sweet honey-pot ants. These were a great treat.

The men were good hunters. They used spears to bring down geese, emus and kangaroos. Some Aborigines used a boomerang with which to kill flying birds, and snakes were often caught by hand. They brought the food back to camp where it was cooked and shared out. Poisonous plants were made safe for eating by either washing or fermenting, which means letting their fruit become over-ripe.

The Aborigines belonged to groups that spoke different languages. There were nearly five hundred of these language groups scattered over Australia. Because Australia is such a big country, the weather is different from place to place. In the hot, dry parts, people lived under shelters made of grass or tree branches. In the colder parts, the huts were made of branches covered with bark, which was held down by rocks.

Some Aborigine families moved home every six months to search for food and water. Others had to move nearly every week. There were no borders or fences, but each group knew exactly where their land began and where it ended. They only took what they needed from the land and they didn't waste food. The land was precious. The Dreaming Spirits had prepared it for them and the Aborigines knew how to look after it. This was so for thousands of years.

Hunting

The young man stood all alone in the clearing. It was late afternoon and the sun was going down. The only sounds were the birds and small animals rustling about in the nearby bushes. Slowly, the man lifted his arm and ran a few steps. Then he threw a curved stick downwards so that it swept through the air at great speed. It twisted and spun, catching the light as it flew. Then, as the man watched, the stick made a wide circle in the sky, and soon it was on its way back towards him.

The 'come-back' boomerang is a short, wooden throwing stick. The boomerang has a curve near the middle and on each side of the curve there's a twist which makes it turn in the air. It takes practice to work this kind of boomerang, which was first used as a kind of toy to show off a man's skill in throwing.

Most boomerangs were not meant to come back. They were one of the Aborigines' main hunting weapons. A hunter would hold one end and hurl the stick at an animal. Once it was in the air, the boomerang turned over and over and hit either the animal or the ground just in front of it – then hit the animal on the first bounce.

Only the older boys and men went hunting. They didn't use many weapons, just their throwing sticks, clubs and spears. The spears could be thrown a long way with spear throwers called woomeras.

Before using their weapons, Aborigines had to track the animals. This meant silently following them until they could creep near enough to make the kill.

Aborigines join in a ceremonial dance. Their bodies are decorated with painted designs and they often wear fine head-dresses.

Come to the corroboree!

Thud, thud. Clap, clap. The silence is broken by hand-clapping and the noise of sticks beaten on the ground. Then the high chant of a man's voice joins in. Next comes the drone of a long wooden tube played like a huge pipe. It gives a low ghostly moan. The music gets faster and faster and the clapping gets louder. Suddenly, a group of dancers leap into the middle of the circle. Their bodies are covered in strange patterns painted with clay. As the music gets faster, the dancers twist and twirl and spin to the beat.

This is an Aboriginal camp ceremony, often called a corroboree. Camp ceremonies were very important for the Aborigines and there were many different kinds. At these ceremonies the Aborigines would meet up with members of their family or people from different groups they hadn't seen for years. Music, song and dance were all part of the camp ceremony. The long tube used to make the droning music is called a didjeridu. It's a hollow, wooden pipe made from a straight branch and can be almost two metres long. It was first used in the north. The didjeridu is played by blowing down the mouth end of the tube and this gives a low, soft note. Some didjeridus are decorated with painted patterns, just like the ones on the dancers.

Ceremonies were held for many different reasons. Some were secret and religious and were for men or women only. Others were held to keep Aboriginal legends alive. And some were held just for fun. Then everyone was allowed to join in.

The dancers twist and stamp to the sound of the didjeridu. This is a long, hollow, wooden tube decorated with patterns.

An Aborigine puts the finishing touches to a bark painting.

Aboriginal art

The artist hunches over his work. He lifts his brush once more and dabs on a touch of brilliant red colour. Then he leans back to look at his painting. It is the outline of a kangaroo filled with exciting shapes and patterns. Yellow, black, red and white lines dance about before his eyes, bringing the picture to life. The painting is magnificent.

Aborigines made pictures on all kinds of surfaces. They painted on the walls of rock shelters, on pieces of tree bark, on their own bodies, and even on the ground. The Arnhem Land Aborigines are known for their bark paintings, which show animals, patterns or scenes from everyday life. Sometimes they made pictures showing the bones of animals, fish and human beings, which is why we call them 'X-ray pictures'. Their painting tools were things they found around them. A stick chewed at one end made a good brush. So did some human hair tied to a twig. Red, yellow and white clays and charcoal were used for paint. Beeswax or turtles' eggs helped the paint to stick.

Many paintings were about the legends and beliefs of the Aborigines.

Kangaroos leap across the walls in this lively cave painting.

The land and the people

The old men led the boy to the secret cave.

It was cool and dark under the rock, but the boy felt hot and sticky and a bit scared.

He looked up and on the wall was a huge painting of a snake. Suddenly, one of the men grabbed hold of the boy's hand and moved it round the curves of the painted snake's body. As his hand traced the picture, the boy listened to the story of the snake, and he felt as if his body, too, was slithering and sliding.

Aboriginal people had no writing. All their stories and beliefs were passed on by word of mouth. They learned by heart all they were told by their teachers. And to help their memories, they drew the shapes of the things they learned about. When the right time came, the young men were told the secret stories. And in this way the important ideas of their religion were kept alive.

Today, many Aboriginal people still keep to their religion. Their religion concerns the Dreaming. It is about what happened in the beginning, and it still has lessons for today. It tells of nature and the land, and of the part human beings have to play in keeping life going well. And it is about the Dreaming Spirits who left part of their own spirit in the places they visited. At birth a child is linked to one of these spirit-places. In that way, all Aborigines have strong ties with the land and what it contains. That is why the land is so important to Aborigines – it is a special part of them.

Aborigines in danger

The Aborigines arrived at their sacred meeting place and were surprised to see the newcomers there. They looked at the cleared ground and at the cutting tools which the Europeans were using. As some of them moved forward curiously to touch the tools, the Europeans shouted out, grabbing back their belongings. They thought that the Aborigines might steal their things! Before long, a skirmish had broken out.

This was just the kind of misunderstanding that used to happen between the Aborigines and the early settlers in Australia. The first Europeans arrived in Australia in 1788. Some of them were convicts from Britain. As the new settlers arrived, they wanted land for their cattle, and ground in which to grow their crops. Soon, they had set up settlements without asking the Aborigines. They cut down trees and built houses for themselves.

Sometimes, the settlers disturbed Aboriginal sacred places. Sometimes, their sheep and cattle interfered with Aboriginal hunting. Soon, fighting broke out and many people were killed. The fighting continued for about a hundred years. But the Aborigines with their wooden spears were no match for the Europeans with their guns.

The Europeans also brought diseases with them, such as measles and influenza, which killed large numbers of Aborigines.

Some of the Aborigines who survived carried on much as before, while others were made to change their way of life to fit in with the Europeans.

Children try to solve a question on the board in a small school in the outback.

Aborigines today

Rosie is an Aboriginal girl and she lives in northern Australia. Rosie lives with her mother, father and brothers and sisters in a house on a cattle station. Lots of other Aboriginal families live there too, so there are plenty of children for Rosie to play with.

Rosie goes to a school that teaches children in both the Aboriginal way and the European way. At school she paints pictures like the ones her people have painted for hundreds of years and she has lessons in an Aboriginal language. She also learns maths and English.

When Rosie isn't in school, she helps her sisters and her mother collect food from the countryside. Sometimes they catch fish and big lizards and eat fruit from the trees. The men often go out hunting kangaroos and wild bullocks with shotguns and rifles. Food such as sugar, flour, salt and tinned fruit is delivered from the town every two weeks in a truck.

At ceremony time, Rosie's father and the other men use the radio to call people together. Children aren't allowed to go to all the ceremonies, but when they do join in they have fun singing and dancing. Rosie learns about the Dreaming from the older people.

But not all Aborigines live like Rosie. Many now live in cities, towns and farming areas of southern Australia. Some have become lawyers and clergy, and a few members of parliament. Notable Aboriginal sporting personalities include the tennis star Evonne Goolagong and a number of footballers. Many are still poor, however. For these people, getting education and employment are two very big problems.

Aborigines today want to make decisions for themselves, and they want to be seen as different from other Australians. As in the past, the land is very important to them. They would like to use and live on their own land. But for many Aborigines, there is still a long struggle ahead.

At work on a cattle station.

The Great Southern Land

In the middle of the 16th century, a new land appeared on French maps. It was called Iave La Grande (Great Java) and it was shown spreading south from Java. But no one seemed to know anything about this new country. It was a mystery. What was it like there? Were there great riches for the taking like gold, silver and jewels? Did strange creatures live there? What were the people like?

Since ancient times, many people had had some idea that a Great Southern Land existed, but no one could really be sure. Between 1271 and 1295, an Italian, Marco Polo, spent many years in China and travelled throughout the Far East. Some stories say he returned to Europe telling of a huge, rich land full of gold, several hundred kilometres south of Java.

Iave La Grande was probably seen by the Portuguese in the 1520s. From that time some maps carried the Portuguese word *Abrolhos*, meaning 'keep your eyes open" off the dangerous Western Australian coast. Some people think that a mahogany wreck buried in sandhills near Warrnambool in Victoria is all that is left of a Portuguese ship, which mapped the entire eastern coast of Australia. Others are not so sure, because nobody can now find the wreck. But sailors went on searching.

We do know that a Dutchman called Willem Jansz saw and named part of Australia's coast in 1605-1606.

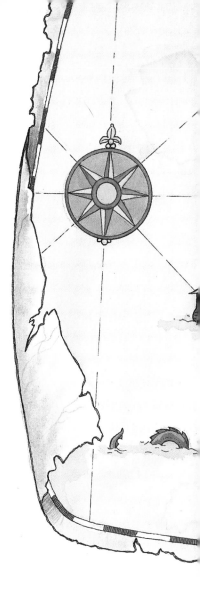

Jansz had set off in his little ship called the Duyfken to map New Guinea. Instead, he arrived at Cape York Peninsula. His sailors returned with terrible tales of hostile people, and said the countryside was flat and bleak.

Little by little, the Great Southern Land became real for the Europeans. At last, it was not just a map-maker's dream, but a continent waiting to be explored.

In the middle of the 16th century, a new land appeared on French maps. It was called lave la Grande.

Stories of the discoverers

The discovery of the huge island of Australia is made up of the stories of men from different European countries.

One of these early discoverers was a Dutchman called Dirck Hartog. At that time, the Dutch had begun sailing a new, faster route to the East Indies, which brought them near the west coast of Australia. In 1616, Dirck Hartog was following this route when he was carried by winds, known as the 'Roaring Forties', to an island in Shark Bay, Western Australia. Hartog scratched his story on a pewter plate and nailed it to a post on the island where it was found eighty years later.

Soon, other Dutch ships made landings in Australia. In 1623, Jan Carstenz and Dirck Melizoon explored the northern coast in two small ships called the Pera and the Arnhem.
Carstenz wrote a report of the journey, saying that the land they'd seen was flat, dry and bare. On the way home, sailors in the Arnhem discovered the part of North Australia we know today as Arnhem Land.

The first Europeans to die in Australia were mutineers on the Dutch ship Batavia, sailing under François Pelsaert. In 1629, the ship hit a reef in a storm, and Pelsaert struggled to help survivors and to search for water. He went off in an open boat several thousand kilometres to Java to get help.

Meanwhile, some of the crew believed he'd never come back and they began to mutiny. They got drunk on casks of wine and decided to take over the ship. These mutineers then broke open chests full of beautifully embroidered suits which the ship was carrying, dressed themselves up, and armed themselves with great knives and cutlasses. Then they began to attack all those who disagreed with them. Months of violence followed, and 125 people were killed.

At last Pelsaert returned and captured the ringleader, Cornelius, and his followers. They were taken to Seal Island, where they were hanged.

Abel Janzoon Tasman, another Dutchman, hoped to find marvellous riches in Australia. He set sail in 1642 with a shipload of fine cloth and silk to trade with the natives. He had two ships, the Zeehaen and the Heemskerck. But he returned home disappointed. He hadn't found the treasure he had hoped would be there. And he told frightening tales of how hostile the natives were. However, he did land on the island which is now named after him, Tasmania. His second voyage was unsuccessful, too. But Tasman did prove that the long coastline from the Gulf of Carpentaria to Exmouth Gulf was part of one piece of land.

The Dutch called it New Holland.

The pirate explorer

How would you like to have a place named
after you? If you look at a map of Australia, in
the north-western corner, you will find some
places named after an Englishman called
William Dampier. There's Dampier Land,
Dampier Bay and a group of small islands
called Dampier Archipelago. William Dampier
visited this part of Australia in 1688 and 1699.
He wrote about the Aborigines and the strange
wildlife he found there.

Dampier's life was a lively one. He was an
explorer and a writer of exciting sea stories.
He even sailed around the world three times.
As a young man, he was a buccaneer.

In January 1688 William Dampier was on board the buccaneer ship Cygnet when it landed in north-western Australia. The ship stopped here for two months for repairs and cleaning. While he was waiting, Dampier made many notes on the plants and animals he saw. He tried to get to know the Aborigines, but they refused to fetch and carry for him, and he lost interest in them.

Back in England, Dampier wrote a book called 'A New Voyage Round the World'. People were fascinated by this exciting record of the faraway lands Dampier had visited. But he didn't enjoy his time in Australia. He wrote that it was a very dry and sandy place, with no fruits or berries to eat.

Dampier returned to Australia eleven years later, this time in command of a ship belonging to the British navy, the HMS Roebuck. The Roebuck reached the western coast of Australia after seven months. The crew spent some time searching for fresh water at Shark Bay, but they found none. They did manage to get some food - the meat from sharks, turtles and kangaroo rats, which Dampier called racoons. The crew, who'd been living on hard biscuits and salted meat, were very glad of the change. The sailors then went further north to look for water. They tried digging wells, but had no luck, so Dampier was forced to set sail.

Botany Bay

When the scientists on board the Endeavour landed at Botany Bay, they found many plants and creatures which they had never seen before. They carefully drew and labelled each one.

"Land ahead!" came the excited cry from Zachary Hicks, the officer on watch. Those who could, rushed to catch sight of the coastline. It was April 20th 1770, and the east coast of Australia had been sighted by white men, possibly for the very first time.

The crew on board the three-masted ship were sailing under their captain, James Cook. The ship was called the Endeavour and had set sail in August 1768, from Plymouth in England. It carried ninety-four people, and food and water for a long voyage. Cook's job was to take a group of scientists to Tahiti to watch the planet Venus cross in front of the sun. But he had another job to do, too. When the work in Tahiti was finished, he had top secret orders to sail further, to find out more about the mysterious Great Southern Land, as Australia was then called.

Endeavour's landing place on April 29th 1770 was an open bay where the crew stayed for eight days. The sailors had a busy time. They searched for food, and gathered oysters, mussels and fish. They managed to catch some giant stingrays, and Cook's first name for the landing place was Sting Ray's Harbour But later he changed his mind because of all the discoveries made by the botanists.

These scientists were full of excitement over the strange new plants and flowers all around them. They rushed about collecting samples and making drawings of what they'd seen. And Cook decided to record the importance of these exciting discoveries by calling the place Botany Bay.

The wonderful collection

The great cabin was lined with pots, bottles, glass jars and boxes of all shapes and sizes. Fishing nets and fish-hooks were scattered everywhere. In the middle of all this, one man sat writing far into the night. His name was Joseph Banks and he was so delighted with his discoveries he couldn't wait to record them.

Joseph Banks and his assistants had joined James Cook when he sailed from England on the Endeavour in 1768. Banks was a naturalist who studied plants and animals, and he'd come on this expedition well-prepared. He'd brought all kinds of equipment to help in his studies – a type of telescope for looking at the seabed, strange machines for catching insects, bottles and boxes for carrying seeds, and jars for keeping animals and plants. The artists who'd come to help Banks would copy his finds on to paper. Banks hoped to make a record of all the strange new plants and animals he met on the long voyage.

He wasn't disappointed. When the party reached the east coast of Australia, they were amazed at the colourful wild plants and unusual animals. They'd never seen anything like it before! They collected hundreds of specimens of seeds, insects, birds and fish. Each one was labelled and sketched.

Imagine the interest Banks's collection caused when he arrived back in England in 1771. The seeds, plants, shells, insects, notes, drawings and bottles of specimens were taken to his house in London. And Joseph Banks's fascinating collection was the talk of the town.

sacred kings fisher

lyrebird

emu

black flying
possum

black swan

flax plant

kangaroo

dingo

The Endeavour River

One clear, summer night Cook's ship Endeavour struck a coral reef. With a hole in her side, the ship began to sink. Men ran everywhere, carrying out orders as quickly as they could. They threw heaps of things overboard to lighten the load – oil jars, caskets, stores and six huge guns. Just as quickly, they plugged up the leak with some old rope, handfuls of wool and a piece of sail cloth. What would happen to them if the ship went down?

But by their hard work, the crew just managed to save Endeavour. They sailed the damaged ship to the beach and dragged her up the bank near a river to begin repairs. Cook called this spot Endeavour River.

Cook's crew stayed at Endeavour River for six weeks to repair the ship. The natural historians were glad of a chance to study the new land further. The plants, flowers, birds and animals were all unusual and fascinating. They caught the first kangaroo ever seen by a white man, and also recorded a flying fox and an opossum with two young. They met some Aborigines who seemed very strange to the Englishmen because they wore bones through their noses and painted their bodies with wild patterns.

At last Endeavour was ready to sail again. This time Cook made sure they sailed clear of the dangerous coral reef. They moved on up the coast to the northern tip, which Cook named Cape York. Near this point, Cook went ashore and raised the British flag at Possession Island. They then made for home.

Cook's party had explored the whole eastern coast of Australia, which Cook called New South Wales because it reminded him of the Welsh coastline. The crew of Endeavour arrived back in England on July 13th 1771, and were welcomed as heroes.

Aboard the Fleet

The man's eyes flicked open with a start. It was dark and stuffy - where was he? Then he remembered, he was on his way to New South Wales! From where he was lying in his hammock, he could just make out the shadowy figure of the guard on watch. He could feel the slow roll of the ship on the waves, and hear the other men coughing and snuffling in the darkness. He wondered what his life would be like from now on.

This man was a convict on board the Prince of Wales transport ship in 1787. It was one of eleven ships making up the First Fleet, which sailed from England to set up the first convict settlement in New South Wales. The idea was to take some of the criminals - both men and women - away from the already overflowing English prisons and set them to work building the new English colony in New South Wales.

Life on board ship was unpleasant. The 760 convicts of the First Fleet were only allowed up on deck for fresh air and exercise when the weather was fine. The rest of the time they were cooped up below, watched by armed guards. The voyage lasted for eight months.

Most of the convicts sent to Australia were thieves and pickpockets. Others were poachers. Almost half of them had to stay in Australia for seven years, but some of the prisoners were sent there for the rest of their lives. Even those who served their time could seldom afford the fare home.

Sydney Cove

"Hip, hip hooray!" The last of the cheers rang out, shots were fired and the British flag was raised while the soldiers stood to attention. It was January 26th 1788, and Governor Phillip's official party was celebrating the beginning of the first British settlement of Australia. Governor Phillip and the hundreds of people who had sailed with him in the First Fleet, had reached Sydney Cove. For many people, it was to become a new home.

This old painting is called the 'Founding of Australia'. It records the landing at Sydney Cove in 1788.

But there was plenty of work to do first. On the second day, Governor Phillip began organizing the building of the settlement. There were tents to put up, stores to be brought ashore, and a lot of clearing to be done, as the shore was covered with trees. Some of the male convicts were brought out from the ships to begin the work. It was the first time they'd set foot on firm ground for many months.

Governor Phillip was worried they'd all go short of food. He knew they must sow some corn as soon as possible. So, from the beginning, he made plans for the layout of the new settlement – where to build and where to farm. Next, the animals from the ships were brought ashore. Many had died on the long journey, but the settlers had cows, sheep, and goats, hens and pigs to join them in their new settlement. Some boats were sent out to fish – and came back with a good catch. Everyone was very busy.

The Governor sent off an exploring party, who had their first meeting with the Aborigines. They were very interested in the Europeans' clothes. They thought they were some sort of extra skin, and were surprised to see that the white people could take them off! But the Aborigines seemed friendly, and even helped the settlers to drag their catches of fish ashore. In return, the settlers gave them some fish.

On the fourth day, after many trees had been cleared, a large frame was carried on to the shore. It was covered with canvas and set up on the east side of the cove. This was Governor Phillip's tent – Australia's first Government House.

Governor Phillip and the Aborigines

The Aborigine walked slowly along with the Englishmen, looking about him with wide eyes. At the Governor's house, someone touched a bell that hung over the door. The Aborigine jumped in fright at the noise – and then began to laugh. Everything in the new, white man's settlement was strange and surprising to the Aborigines.

Bennelong explains the use of the boomerang to some important guests.

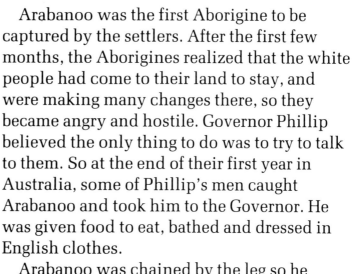

Arabanoo was the first Aborigine to be captured by the settlers. After the first few months, the Aborigines realized that the white people had come to their land to stay, and were making many changes there, so they became angry and hostile. Governor Phillip believed the only thing to do was to try to talk to them. So at the end of their first year in Australia, some of Phillip's men caught Arabanoo and took him to the Governor. He was given food to eat, bathed and dressed in English clothes.

Arabanoo was chained by the leg so he wouldn't run away, and the settlers tried to speak with him. For a while, Arabanoo was quiet and gloomy, but slowly he began to get to know the white people. He learned some English words and taught the English the Aboriginal names for things. Sadly, Arabanoo was only with the settlers for five months before he caught smallpox and died. Governor Phillip had been very fond of the Aborigine, and buried Arabanoo in his garden.

Governor Phillip was a kind and good man. He was always friendly towards the Aborigines. He also tried to be fair and just to the convicts. After Arabanoo, the Governor captured two more Aborigines, called Colbee and Bennelong. They both escaped, but afterwards Bennelong went back to the settlers and became friendly with them. He was very popular with the white men, and was taken to England to meet King George III. A part of Sydney Harbour is named after Bennelong, in memory of his friendliness towards the settlers. It is Bennelong Point, where Sydney Opera House now stands.

Experiment Farm

Another day began for James Ruse and, as usual, the first thing he did was to kneel on the ground and peer at the soil. But this day was different. "Yes!" he shouted, "I've done it!"

For Ruse could see the first shoots of wheat and maize pushing through the earth. He was able to say he was one of the first farmers in New South Wales.

But James Ruse hadn't always been a farmer. He'd arrived in Australia with the First Fleet in 1788, a convict jailed for house-breaking. He was sentenced to seven years. But his behaviour was good, and after his sentence, he was given his freedom.

At this time the colony of New South Wales was in trouble – it was short of food. Farming had been unsuccessful and very few crops had grown. Ruse knew something about farming, and he was asked to see what he could do. A bargain was struck up – Ruse was sent to farm at Rose Hill, a place near Parramatta, and if he succeeded he could have a farm of his own.

James Ruse worked hard on the land, turning over the earth, hoeing, digging and spreading ashes on to the soil. In May 1790 he sowed wheat and in August he planted maize. He also made a vegetable garden. Just over a year later, he was able to feed himself and his family on what he'd grown.

The bargain was kept and Ruse was granted his land – called Experiment Farm. He did well here too, and later moved on to another farm on the Hawkesbury River. It wasn't long before he was growing wheat to sell at the Government Stores in Sydney.

James Ruse had shown what could be done, so other ex-convicts were granted land for their own farms too.

Governor Macquarie

The tall, dark-haired man stood on the deck of the sailing ship. There were no other ships in the port, so he had a good view of the land in front of him. He could see rows of crooked buildings, a couple of bridges and roads, and a few scattered gum trees behind. He was looking at almost all of the little settlement he had come to govern.

It was New Year's Day in 1810 and Governor Lachlan Macquarie had come to rule over the convict settlement at Sydney, in New South Wales. The settlement was almost twenty-two years old. Macquarie had more power here than the King of England, because he had no advisors to help him. He would have to make all the decisions on his own. He looked forward to the challenge of being a good and wise governor.

Macquarie set about his job quickly. At the time, Sydney was full of dangerous, narrow streets. The houses were plain and shabby. Macquarie decided to tidy up the town. He built new streets, houses, a church and a hospital. Then he made sure the roads were better and safer.

While the building was going on, Governor Macquarie got to know some of the prisoners living in his settlement. He looked back to the work of Sydney's very first governor, Captain Arthur Phillip. And, like Phillip, Macquarie decided to help those who had served their prison sentences. He gave jobs in the law courts to two ex-convicts, and he invited others to dinner at his house.

Governor Macquarie was a keen explorer. He went on journeys himself and encouraged parties of men to make longer expeditions to find new farming land. The line of mountains with high cliffs had stopped settlers finding new land for twenty-six years. But under Macquarie, the ridge called the Blue Mountains was crossed by white men for the first time. Macquarie felt proud of the victory.

In 1814, a party of thirty convict labourers and eight soldiers were busy building a road. It followed the tracks of the explorers. They managed to build more than 160 kilometres in only six months. After all their hard work, Macquarie rewarded the road-builders with their freedom.

By the time Governor Macquarie left Sydney to return to Britain, he had made many changes. Sydney had become quite a beautiful town. The settlement had discovered new areas of land for building and farming. No other governor was as popular with the convict settlers. In fact, Macquarie was one of the best governors ever sent to Australia.

The convict architect

The two men stood side by side and looked up at the building. The brand-new lighthouse rose above them, perched on a high cliff top. And hundreds of metres below, the flat, blue sea stretched away to the horizon. The building was called Macquarie's Tower – and it was beautiful.

One of the men felt specially proud at the sight of the lighthouse. His name was Francis Greenway and he'd planned the building. The whole shape and size had been worked out by him – down to the smallest window. To be standing in front of something you'd begun in pencil on a piece of paper was a wonderful feeling.

The other man was pleased too. He was Governor Macquarie, and the lighthouse had been named after him. He turned to Greenway to thank him.

The Governor gave more than his thanks – he gave a pardon, which meant freedom. For Greenway was a convict. He'd been sent to the convict colony in New South Wales for a type of cheating called forgery. But he'd worked well there, and after a while, the Governor made him Civil Architect. His job was to plan buildings for the town of Sydney.

Greenway and Governor Macquarie worked well together. Macquarie was interested in building, and Greenway was good at his job. Between them, they worked on churches, houses, bridges and roads. Soon Greenway had planned some of Australia's first buildings. And he was able to watch his designs come to life all around him.

The tyrant of Moreton Bay

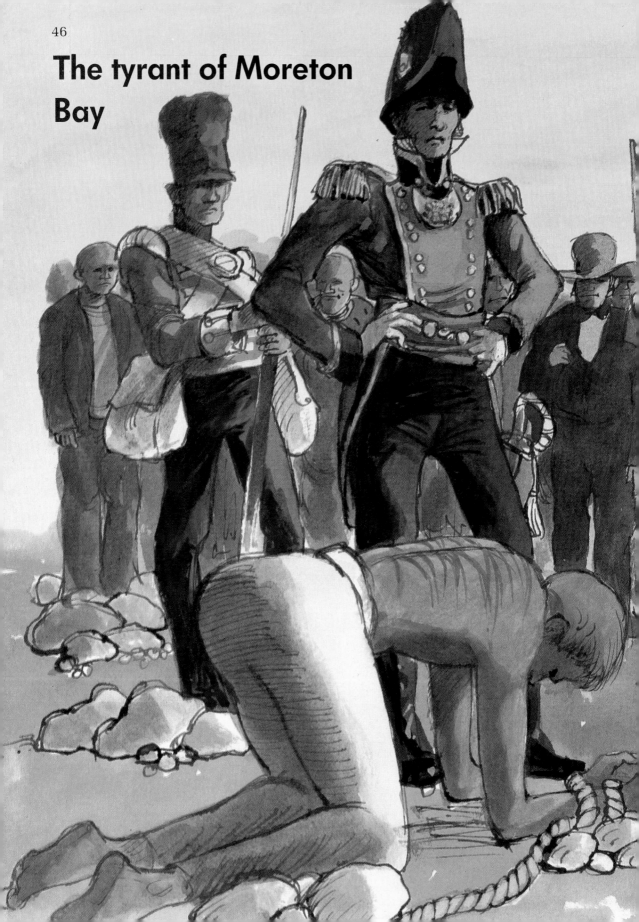

Captain Patrick Logan was in charge of the colony of convicts at Moreton Bay. And he made sure the men knew it! If any man didn't do a job properly or grumbled at the task, Logan would punish him with a flogging. One prisoner was sentenced to three hundred lashes! Captain Logan was feared by many.

Logan believed in hard work. Prisoners were kept at tasks from sunrise to sunset. They had to build, carry, dig, and drag timber and rocks. They were only allowed short breaks for breakfast and dinner. Hard farming work was all done by hand until the men felt their backs would break. There were no ploughs. The food was poor and gave them little energy. Tough, salted meat turned green in the hot summer months and the hard biscuits were full of beetles called weevils. No wonder so many men tried to run away from the Moreton Bay colony! They were sure that nowhere else could be so bad.

Many of the convicts may have planned to get their revenge on Logan, but it was probably the Aborigines who put an end to his rule. Logan went on an expedition with a party of explorers and never returned. He was later found lying in a simple grave, partly covered by earth, on the bank of the river. He had been beaten on the head and murdered.

Captain Logan had done a lot of good work at the colony. He had set up many new buildings and improved the farming. But by some people he would always be remembered as the tyrant of Moreton Bay.

The convict businesswoman

"Wake up!" shouted the judge. Mary jumped. "Stop day-dreaming and listen to your sentence. Is it true that you stole a horse?"

"Yes, sir!" said Mary.

"And is it true that you went dressed as a boy, calling yourself James Burrow?"

"Yes, sir!" said Mary again.

"Then you will be transported to Sydney in New South Wales for seven years."

Mary was only thirteen when she was sent to Australia for horse-stealing. When she arrived in Sydney, she began work as a nursemaid in a large house.

On the way to Australia, Mary met a young Irishman called Thomas Reibey. Two years later, they were married. Thomas Reibey was a businessman and a farmer. He traded in grain and other goods, and he owned ships, too. Then Thomas died. Mary Reibey was still a young woman. She was a mother of seven children and found herself with many businesses to run.

Mary got on with the work at once. She had often looked after things for Thomas when he had been away. Now she bought more ships, farms and buildings in the city.

Mary was busy in other ways, too. She was interested in the church and in charities. Soon, she was made one of the governors of the Grammar School.

Mary Reibey became very wealthy. She was known wherever she went in the colony as the successful businesswoman. Life in the new land could be just what you made it.

Buckley's chance

Tired, dirty and hungry, William Buckley scratched about in the bush, searching for something to eat. After a while, he felt he was being watched. Looking up, he saw a crowd of Aborigines staring at him. Buckley felt scared, but he pulled himself up to his full height and smiled at the men. They looked again at the huge white man, and moved forward to welcome him.

William Buckley was an escaped convict. He'd been sent to Australia for dealing in stolen goods. As soon as he got to Port Phillip Bay settlement, he made up his mind to escape. He crossed the bay and hid in a cave until he felt it was safe to move.

Buckley's biggest worry was how to find food in the rough countryside. It was lucky for him he met the Aborigines. Buckley was a big man – tall and well-built. And to the Aborigines he seemed to be an ancestor come back from the dead, for their law told them that returning ancestors would be white. So they made friends with him and welcomed him to share their life in the bush.

Buckley settled down well to his new life. He learned to eat the roots and small animals he found in the bush. And he learned the Aborigines' language. When he went back to the white men after thirty-two years, he'd almost forgotten how to speak English. He'd become the wild white man of the bush.

Convict life

It was 7.30 in the morning and already the man was tired. He was wet too, for he'd been working up to his waist in water since daybreak. All he had to look forward to was a bowl of watery porridge called skilly.

This was the life of a convict working on the building of a jetty in Macquarie Harbour, Tasmania, in the 1820s. It was a penal colony, a place where prisoners who'd committed serious crimes after arriving in Australia were sent for special punishment. Life there was very hard indeed, and to be sent there brought fear to a man's heart. But only about one man in every twenty was sent to a place like this.

Many more prisoners in Australia worked as farm labourers or were set more pleasant building tasks. Some convicts might even work as private school teachers or servants,

and live almost as one of the family in a rich settler's home. Even so, in the early days there were many rules which the prisoner was not allowed to break and he had very little freedom. For a wrongdoing, his 'master' could take him to be beaten or put in an iron gang, where he'd be chained up and made to work at jobs like road-making.

After serving several years of his sentence, a well-behaved prisoner could get a 'ticket of leave'. This meant he could work for himself, so long as he reported to the police regularly and didn't do anything wrong. If he kept this up, he might then be given a conditional pardon – which meant he was free, but was not allowed to go back to England.

There was also a chance to earn a completely free pardon, which meant he'd be as free as anyone else. Under this system, many ex-convicts were able to build new lives for themselves in a brand-new land.

The inland explorers

Earth hard as rock, rivers all dried up and the sun forever beating down. The smell of food rotting in the heat, and the buzz of flies.

Or the deadly bogs, waiting to trap a man and suck him under. Then the tramping, day after day, until your legs ached and your feet bled.

All this was part of life for some of Australia's early explorers.

Why did they do it? Why did these men face the horrors of the hard landscape, when they knew what lay ahead? And why did some go on three or four of these nightmare journeys?

The early settlers in Australia needed to explore to find new land. It was needed for farming and for grazing sheep and cattle.

As time went on, people thought more and more about those parts of Australia where no white man had yet been. Perhaps there were green pastures there, watered by great rivers. So the governors of the settlements sent explorers to find out.

These inland explorers were brave men. They knew what terror such a journey might bring. But they also saw the undiscovered country as a challenge. For them the wild, high ridges and the flat, bare deserts were all part of Australia's mystery. They wanted to find out what was beyond these unfriendly places. And they were determined to be the first to do it.

Across the Blue Mountains

Day after day, the small group of men stumbled across the rocky landscape. Sometimes they managed ten kilometres, some days only five, because their way was blocked by thick bushes and trees. They clung to the tops of ridges and marked their path by burning the bark of trees as they went along. Sometimes the men were so tired they found it hard to walk.

Four worn-out pack-horses staggered alongside the men. With a sudden crash, one of the horses dropped to its knees in the dust. With the last of their energy, the explorers tore branches from the trees and used them to help raise the tired animal to its feet.

The men of this exploring party were Gregory Blaxland, William Lawson and William Wentworth. They were travelling with four convicts, five dogs and four pack-horses carrying supplies. Their aim was to cross the high Blue Mountains to find new farmland. Many people had tried to cross the mountain range before, but they'd failed. Following the valleys only brought them up against high cliffs and rock faces which they couldn't climb. Now, in 1813, Blaxland, Lawson and Wentworth had a different plan — to follow the ridges. From there they could look down on the land below.

After many days, the weary explorers found themselves in a grassy meadow. The men rested and feasted on fish from the river and on a kangeroo caught by the dogs. The horses had all the grass they could munch.

And later, from the top of a mountain peak, Blaxland's party saw the rich grasslands of the western plains. It was time to return to Sydney with the good news.

Blaxland's party had shown how to cross the Blue Mountains. They had pointed the way to rich new land, just right for settlement.

Finding the Liverpool Plains

In 1818, John Oxley led an expedition to explore the Macquarie River in Eastern Australia. There were fifteen men in the party, including George Evans the explorer, Charles Fraser the botanist, and Dr John Harris the surgeon. The party took nineteen horses.

Oxley's team marched north along the Macquarie looking for good grazing land for sheep. This was the real purpose of the expedition. But they were soon disappointed. The river ended in a huge marsh where tall reeds waved above the men's heads. Oxley thought that he was getting close to an inland sea in the centre of Australia, but he couldn't find it. After a while, the party left the Macquarie River and turned east. The marshy land was terrible — the men walked up to their waists in water for a long way.

Eventually, Evans came across another river called the Castlereagh. Here, there was nothing but bog. One poor horse rolled into the river. Then all the horses were sinking fast. The men had to cut the loads off the horses' backs before they could be pulled out. The horses were very tired and frightened. They kept lying down around the men, and acted just like dogs!

Then things began to improve. The team came to some hills, and beyond the hills they saw some wonderful land. There were all kinds of animals there, and the dogs were sent to hunt kangaroo. Oxley named the place the Liverpool Plains.

After a while, the team approached the mountains called The Great Dividing Range. Here, they encountered a very deep river valley which proved treacherous for the horses. They slipped and slid over the slopes. Three of them lost their footing and rolled over, but they were saved by some trees.

At last, the explorers reached the coastal side of the mountains. Here, the vegetation was dense and they had to cut their way through some thick vines. It was hard going, and they could only move a short distance in a day. But they found the Hastings River and tracked it down to the sea at a place they named Port Macquarie.

Now the team had to march south along the coast. They found a boat and carried it with them so they could cross any streams which they came across along the way. One day, William Blake, the harness-maker, was speared by an Aborigine. This shook the men. But on arriving home, they were pleased with the discovery of the Liverpool Plains.

Overland to Port Phillip

Imagine scrambling on your hands and knees for hours over hills and ridges. Flies and mosquitoes are darting at your face and neck. It's hot, uncomfortably hot, you are hungry and exhausted, but you know you must go on.

This is what happened to Hamilton Hume and William Hovell on their expedition across unknown land to Port Phillip. They'd set out with a small party of men from the settlement at Lake George, to explore the land between Lake George and the coast. They were successful, but it was a terrible journey.

At one point the party was faced with the Murrumbidgee River, which was about thirty-two metres wide. How would they get their supplies across? After some thought, Hume and Hovell turned one of their carts into a boat! They wrapped a waterproof sheet around it, and using ropes, made a kind of ferryboat which they used to tow their belongings across the water.

The worst part of their journey was at the last high range of mountains that stood

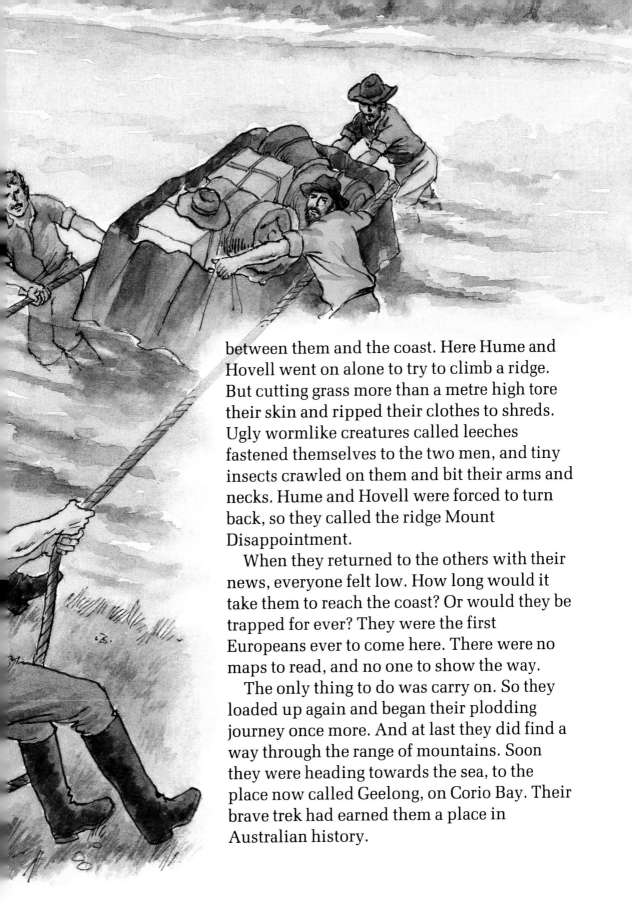

between them and the coast. Here Hume and
Hovell went on alone to try to climb a ridge.
But cutting grass more than a metre high tore
their skin and ripped their clothes to shreds.
Ugly wormlike creatures called leeches
fastened themselves to the two men, and tiny
insects crawled on them and bit their arms and
necks. Hume and Hovell were forced to turn
back, so they called the ridge Mount
Disappointment.

When they returned to the others with their
news, everyone felt low. How long would it
take them to reach the coast? Or would they be
trapped for ever? They were the first
Europeans ever to come here. There were no
maps to read, and no one to show the way.

The only thing to do was carry on. So they
loaded up again and began their plodding
journey once more. And at last they did find a
way through the range of mountains. Soon
they were heading towards the sea, to the
place now called Geelong, on Corio Bay. Their
brave trek had earned them a place in
Australian history.

The riddle of the rivers

The drought was very bad. Sheep were dying from hunger and the wheat wouldn't grow. It was 1828 in New South Wales and the dry weather went on and on.

Governor Darling decided something must be done. What was it like in those parts of Australia where no white man had ever been? Was the land greener there? Wasn't it true that the land was watered by great rivers? The Governor believed Captain Charles Sturt was just the person to find out.

Sturt set off with a party of seven convicts, two soldiers and one free man. Another explorer, Hamilton Hume, went with them. They also had pack-horses, oxen and a boat.

The sun was their enemy. It cracked their lips and the heat brought blisters to their faces. They had other enemies too. Aborigines followed the small party — and one Aborigine was wearing a European coat. Sturt wondered what had happened to the European.

The explorers found two rivers on their journey. Sturt called one of them the Darling.

Later on they came to the dry bed of the
Castlereagh River. Here, things were just as
bad as at home. Trees, plants and animals were
all dying because of the heat. Sturt and Hume
saw large birds called emus struggle for breath
as they searched for water. And Aborigines
begged the white people for food for their
children. The great river had completely
dried up.

Sturt and his tired party returned home.
They had found two rivers, the Bogan and the
Darling, to put on the map. But where the
rivers went was still a mystery
that needed to be solved.

Down the Murrumbidgee

The eight white men huddled together on their boat. Along the riverbanks they could see lines of Aborigines waving sharp-pointed spears. Their dark bodies were painted with red, yellow and white clays. And they chanted war-songs. Suddenly, the boat turned a bend and there stood sixty fierce-looking warriors. The white men got ready to fight for their lives.

Then, on the other bank, a giant Aborigine appeared. He dived into the river and swam across to the warriors. When he reached them, he shook his fists in their faces then he opened his arms to welcome the frightened white men.

This was just one of the adventures that happened during Charles Sturt's second expedition, in 1830. This time he and his men were exploring the Murrumbidgee-Lachlan River system. They were hoping at last to solve the mystery of the rivers that flowed inland, instead of to the ocean.

Sturt found that the Murrumbidgee and Lachlan rivers joined the Murray River, before flowing to the coast. It took them thirty-three days of hard rowing to go 1,600 kilometres along the Murrumbidgee, into the Murray, past the junction of the Darling, and finally to the sea at Lake Alexandrina, to the east of Encounter Bay. Once there they were overjoyed – just like fitting pieces into a jigsaw puzzle, they had filled in the huge empty spaces on the map. And they had recorded a great system of rivers.

The journey back was dreadful. Everyone took turns rowing, for now they had to row against the current. Food was running out and the men were weak. Rain and thick mud made everything worse. By now the party was living on just a little bread and tea. Their bodies were thin and their arms and legs stuck out like sticks. Sometimes they fell asleep at the oars, tired and ill from lack of food.

The explorers did manage to get back to Sydney. Sturt went blind for months afterwards because of the terrible time he'd had. But the riddle of the rivers had been solved and a new stretch of land had been discovered. This would prove to be rich and fertile land, ideal for the settlers to raise their sheep and cattle.

Australia Felix

Thomas Mitchell looked at the small pond. His men needed fish to eat, but the pond was cloudy.

"I'll dive in and see what I can catch," said John Piper, one of Mitchell's party. So Mitchell and a few others stood on the bank and waited. Soon Piper was pulling himself out of the filthy water with something on the end of his fishing-spear. It wasn't a fish at all – it was a human leg! They were clearly in dangerous country – it was time to move on!

This happened during Thomas Livingstone Mitchell's most successful expedition. His exploring party was checking out the river system in New South Wales. Mitchell had twenty-four men with him, dressed in red woollen shirts and white braces to make them look like soldiers. The man called John Piper was an Aborigine who spoke English, and who could help Mitchell understand any Aborigines they might meet.

At one point, Piper overheard some Aborigines plotting to capture Mitchell and kill him. They were angry with him for killing some of their people in an earlier fight. Piper

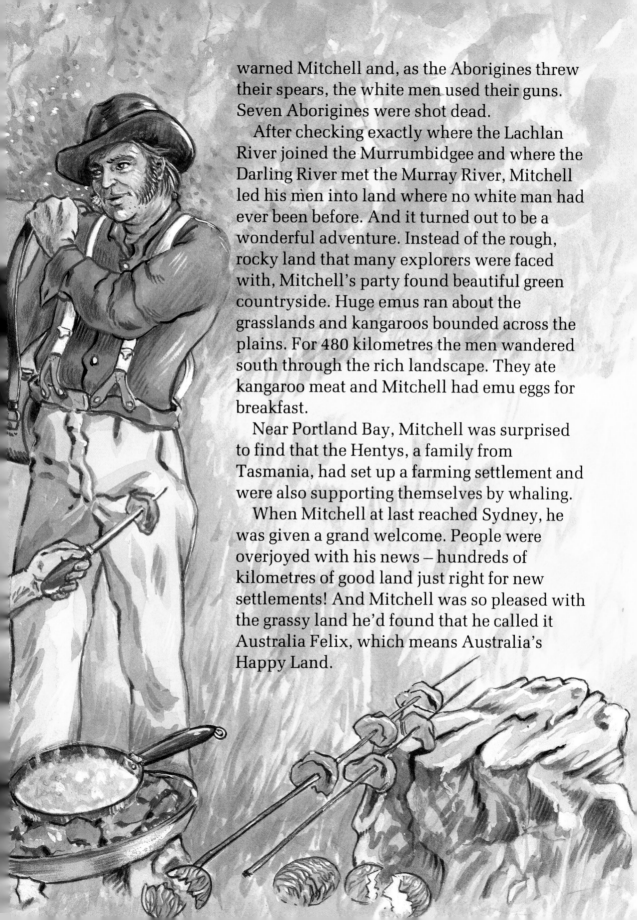

warned Mitchell and, as the Aborigines threw their spears, the white men used their guns. Seven Aborigines were shot dead.

After checking exactly where the Lachlan River joined the Murrumbidgee and where the Darling River met the Murray River, Mitchell led his men into land where no white man had ever been before. And it turned out to be a wonderful adventure. Instead of the rough, rocky land that many explorers were faced with, Mitchell's party found beautiful green countryside. Huge emus ran about the grasslands and kangaroos bounded across the plains. For 480 kilometres the men wandered south through the rich landscape. They ate kangaroo meat and Mitchell had emu eggs for breakfast.

Near Portland Bay, Mitchell was surprised to find that the Hentys, a family from Tasmania, had set up a farming settlement and were also supporting themselves by whaling.

When Mitchell at last reached Sydney, he was given a grand welcome. People were overjoyed with his news – hundreds of kilometres of good land just right for new settlements! And Mitchell was so pleased with the grassy land he'd found that he called it Australia Felix, which means Australia's Happy Land.

Across the Great Australian Bight

One after the other, the horses shot off towards the sea. The men raced after them, yanking them back by the reins. It took all their strength — but how could the poor beasts know that salt water wasn't good for them? They were nearly mad with thirst.

Of course, the men were thirsty, too, and the look of the sea was a torment. They even tried collecting dew to wet their lips. But they had been warned. Others had told them there was no drinking water for 160 kilometres.

These men were an exploring party led by Edward Eyre on their way round the coast of the Great Australian Bight. Three Aborigines and one other white man made up the team. Eyre had failed in his attempt to reach the very centre of Australia the year before. Now he was making a trip round the waterless coast. Although Eyre didn't set out to prove it, this journey showed cattle-owners that there was no safe way around the Bight for their herds. It could hardly be managed by a team of explorers.

It was a terrible journey. The five men of the party were attacked by bloodsucking flies. At one point, Eyre counted twenty-three sitting on his leg at once! In the daytime the heat was unbearable, but at night the temperature fell so low that they shivered with cold.

After a while, two of the Aborigines left the team. But they came back as thieves and robbed Eyre's supplies. John Baxter, the other white man, was killed in the struggle. Now Eyre was alone with just one Aborigine, Wylie, in one of the wildest parts of the country.

They journeyed on for 1,120 kilometres until they found better land. Here, they fed on fish and crabs, kangaroos, wallabies and duck. Then they had the good fortune to find a French whaling boat anchored near the shore. The French gave them food and wine. At last, full and rested, the two were able to finish their journey.

Eyre and Wylie had shown that there wasn't a route for cattle along the Great Australian Bight. The trek of 1,600 kilometres through waterless, unfriendly land had made them Australian heroes.

Eyre and Wylie are lucky enough to spot a French boat during their long, exhausting trek.

The mystery of the disappearing explorer

MISSING! LUDWIG LEICHHARDT, PATHFINDER AND EXPLORER, AGED 34

In 1848, Ludwig Leichhardt, famous for his successful expedition from Brisbane to Port Essington, set out from eastern Australia, where Roma in Queensland is today. With him went a small exploring party of seven men. Their idea was to journey through unknown land across Australia, and down the west coast to Perth. Leichhardt was never seen again. Search parties were sent to find him but failed. After that, all kinds of rumours grew up about the missing explorer. Could any of them be true?

"Leichhardt and his men died of thirst. Then their bodies were swept away when the Barcoo River flooded."

"Leichhardt and his men were all killed by Aborigines. I've spoken to an Aborigine who saw it happen. Afterwards, the natives feasted on Leichhardt's horses."

"Leichhardt's party went to live with Aboriginal people near the Leichhardt River. They all died of fever except one – and he's still alive – somewhere."

"We went to investigate rumours of a wild white man living with Aborigines. We were not able to find anyone of this description. But we did find skeletons and white men's clothing at the Diamantina River. We believe these belonged to some of Leichhardt's party. They may have been killed by Aborigines."

"There's a paradise land right in the middle of Australia. Leichhardt's party got lost there and were captured. Leichhardt's a prisoner."

"Seven skeletons have been found around an old camp fire in the Simpson Desert. I have examined some coins, pieces of bone, a tooth, and some scraps of iron and leather found near the camp. The skeletons may be what's left of Leichhardt and his party."

"I've seen one of Leichhardt's men. He's the only one left alive and he's got an Aboriginal wife. He told me Leichhardt's party mutinied and killed their leader. But then the others were killed themselves by Aborigines."

And the mystery of the disappearing explorer remains unsolved to this day.

Journey to the centre

It was hot at the camp at Depot Glen. The temperature was so high that the ink in the men's pens dried before it touched the paper. The heat pulled the fastening from their boxes. It stopped their hair growing and made their fingernails break off. The party of explorers had never known heat like it.

The leader of the expedition was Captain Charles Sturt. He was now a man of fifty, and a brave and experienced explorer. He was searching for a great inland sea, which many people believed was in the very middle of Australia. He had with him a boat, all ready to sail the waves of his new discovery.

In 1844, they set off towards the centre of the continent. Sturt took four other men with him, some horses, and enough supplies for fifteen weeks. The rest of the party stayed at camp near some water, where they settled the cattle they'd brought along. And one man had a special job to do. He was to get the boat painted, ready for when it would be needed.

Things did not go well for the five travellers. As they went on, the landscape got rougher. There were hundreds of kilometres of sand hills, and a stony desert which cut the horses' hoofs. Great cracks in the dried-up earth made the going dangerous, and still the sun beat down. Sturt knew they were only 240 kilometres from the very heart of Australia. But here nothing was alive, the creeks were drying up fast, and his men were in danger. He gave the order to turn back.

After a rest back at the camp, Sturt decided to try again. This time, Sturt took a small party 160 kilometres east of his first path. But the stony desert stopped them again. It was no good – the dry weather had beaten them. They turned back a second time.

Panting with thirst, they saw small pools of water shrink to nothing under the burning sun. Their thermometer blew up at 53° centigrade. They were only saved from dying by the birds, who dipped to the ground wherever there was a tiny dribble of water or a scrap of meat buried in the sand. By watching the birds, the men found just enough food and water to keep them alive.

Sturt, blackened from the sun, made the end of the journey by cart. He was so weak from disease he couldn't walk. But he'd proved that there was no sea in the centre of Australia. He had left his lovely boat rotting in a dried-out creek.

Race to the coast

As their horses trotted along, the men in the search party looked all about them. Shading their eyes from the glare of the sun, they noticed a group of Aborigines camped in a creek. As soon as the white men approached, one of the Aborigines came forwards and waited. He had a long, dirty beard and tatters for clothes, his skin was burned a dark brown colour. Suddenly the search party knew who he was. He wasn't an Aborigine at all!

The man was John King, one of the men the search party had been looking for. He was filthy and almost too weak to walk – but he was alive! King was the only survivor from the Burke and Wills expedition to the north coast of Australia, and he had a ghastly story to tell.

The expedition had set off in August 1860 with supplies, horses and twenty-six camels, to brave the dry desert in the heart of Australia. The plan was to explore from coast to coast, through the unknown centre. But things had gone wrong from the beginning – the team of explorers had quarrelled, the horses were frightened of the camels, and the party didn't keep together.

Then Robert Burke the leader had news that another explorer was about to make the same journey. From then on Burke saw the expedition as a race. No one was going to beat him to the north! So he split up the party again and took just three men with him – William Wills, who was second in command, John

King and Charles Gray. Leaving the others to camp at Cooper Creek, the four men set out for the coast. They took with them six camels and a pony.

Day after day the small party trudged onwards. The landscape was dusty desert and the heat was terrible. When they managed to find water, it was a strange white colour. But Burke hurried his men along – they must reach the coast.

Then the countryside changed. Now the land was marshy and the going was even harder. Mud and slime were everywhere and the camels sank up to their stomachs in the boggy ground. But nothing could stop Burke. He and Wills went on ahead until a flock of seagulls showed them they'd reached the coast at last.

After all the problems, Burke had succeeded – but it had taken eight weeks. The four men now had enough supplies left for four weeks more. And so they began their horror trip back home.

The Dig tree

Robert Burke stared ahead, then he fired a shot and waited to hear another in answer. How good it would be when he and his two companions reached the camp at Cooper Creek! They would have food and water, clean clothes and they would be safe at last. The two men behind him thought the same as they made their way slowly forward, dragging a camel between them. They were also listening for the answering shot. But it never came. Something must be wrong!

At last Robert Burke, William Wills and John King reached the camp at Cooper Creek. The place was deserted. Their hearts sank. Then Wills saw a message carved on a tree trunk. It said, DIG 3 feet N.W.

The men found the place and dug until they uncovered a bottle. Inside the bottle was a note. It told them that the party had finally decided to leave, after waiting so long. And the note was dated that very day. They had missed each other by hours! Buried with the note were some supplies — flour, rice, sugar, oatmeal and meat.

Burke, Wills and King were shattered. What could they do now? The two camels which were still alive couldn't take another step, and their pony was dead. On the horrific journey back from the coast, Charles Gray's legs had given out and he had died. Now their own legs were almost paralysed. Time was running out.

The exhausted men set out to reach a cattle station at Mount Hopeless, which was about 240 kilometres away, in South Australia.

But the men were very weak. They ended up living by the creek a few kilometres from the deserted camp. Wills wanted to ask the Aborigines for help, but Burke refused. They killed the last camel for food, and from then on they lived on nardoo, a paste made from seeds. When Burke and Wills finally died, their arms and legs were skin and bone.

It was the Aborigines who saved King. When his friends died, they took him to live with them and share their food. And this is how the search party finally found him — thin and weak, but alive to tell the tale of the expedition that went hopelessly wrong.

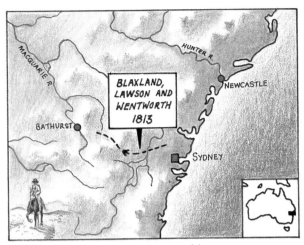

Blaxland's party showed how to cross the Blue Mountains west of Sydney in 1813.

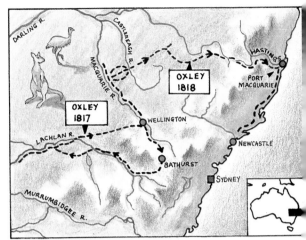

The route taken by John Oxley in 1818 as he explored the Macquarie River in Eastern Australia.
The map also shows his 1817 expedition

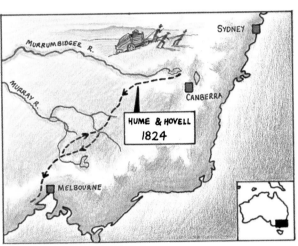

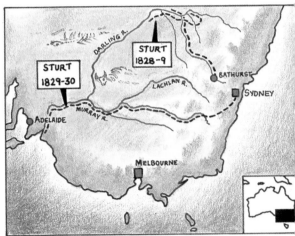

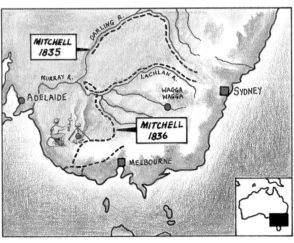

Sturt's journey north-west to the Darling river, and his later expedition along the Murrumbidgee.

Above left
Hamilton Hume and William Hovell's expedition across unknown land to Port Phillip.

Left
Mitchell's exploration in 1836 of the land he called Australia Felix, and his earlier expedition of 1835.

Routes of the explorers

These maps show the routes which the explorers took as they set out on their daring journeys into unknown Australia.

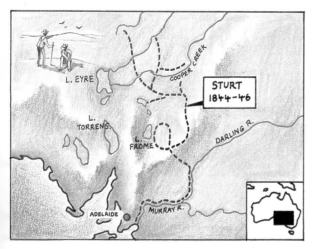

Sturt's trek to the centre of the continent.

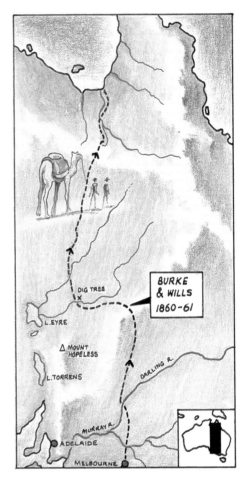

The doomed Burke and Wills expedition to the north coast of Australia.

Eyre's coastal journey around the Great Australian Bight.

Gold at Lewis Ponds Creek

The men bent down carefully and scratched the gravel with their picks. Then they took trowels, dug some earth and put it in a tin dish. Gently, they began to swill it in the waterhole. There, glinting in the pan, was a tiny speck of what they were looking for — gold.

The gold-finders were two men called John Lister and William Tom. They were working with Edward Hargraves, who had learned how to get the gold from the ground in California. Hargraves knew that other diggers from California would follow close behind him, so he went to Sydney to establish his claim. He wanted

the honour of discovering the first gold-field in Australia.

The Californian gold rush had excited many Australians, and there were many rumours of gold being found by shepherds in the mountains near Sydney and Adelaide. Hargraves went to Sydney to negotiate his claim to the gold at the waterhole at Lewis Ponds Creek with the Governor, who wanted to see more gold.

Meanwhile, Lister and Tom were busy digging back at the creek. Hargraves had taught Lister how to pan. The men worked hard, and washed 110 grams of gold. It was enough to prove the place was a gold-field. The gold-field was called Ophir, after the rich gold-mines of King Solomon in the Bible. The first Australian gold rush had begun.

Life on the gold-fields

Bang! Bang! The men fired their shotguns into the air and roared with laughter. Their shot was not the usual lead – but gold nuggets. Another favourite sport was to play skittles – with full champagne bottles. It was Christmas 1853 in the gold-fields and the lucky diggers were enjoying themselves. What was money to them? They'd made their fortunes by digging in the earth, and there was plenty more gold left. One party even ate their Christmas pudding sprinkled with gold!

Life on the gold-fields was noisy, exciting and hard. Many people lived in tents or wooden shacks. Gold-seekers came from almost everywhere – there were businessmen, university students, farmers and merchants all working side by side. The work was dirty and backbreaking. The diggers dug shafts into the ground and brought the gold up mixed with bucketfuls of earth. Later they used a machine called a windlass to help them but, like all their machines, it had to be hand-made. Of course, the hard work of gold digging was a gamble and not all the gold-seekers were lucky. Others made good – but not through digging. They became tradesmen in the busy gold rush areas.

Eureka Stockade

It was blazing hot on the gold-field at Ballarat. A low moaning drifted through the air. It came from a man who was chained to a tree. The fierce afternoon sun was burning his head and arms, but he couldn't get free.

This man had been chained to the tree by police, simply for not having his licence in his pocket. The licence was a piece of paper to show that a digger had paid his fee to work on the gold-fields. Police would go 'digger-hunting', checking everyone's licence. And any who couldn't find it straight away were chained to trees or logs all day or all night.

The diggers were already angry with the government about the licences, and when the licence-hunting was increased to twice a week, they became furious. Anything could happen – and soon it did.

A digger was murdered outside the Eureka Hotel. The diggers believed he'd been killed by James Bentley, the owner. But the chief magistrate, Bentley's friend, declared him innocent. The diggers had a protest meeting, and in the riot that followed, the Eureka Hotel was burned to the ground.

The diggers' leader was an Irishman called Peter Lalor. The diggers were fighting for their freedom. They said they would not be hunted like dogs, and they burned their licences. Then they raised their own flag of blue silk with a huge silver Southern Cross, as a challenge to the government. This was rebellion!

On Saturday December 2nd 1854, the diggers built a stockade of wooden posts at the place called Eureka. They were armed, yet they didn't believe the government forces would attack on a Sunday.

But they did. At dawn the next day the attack came and Lalor's men faced a big fighting force of soldiers and police. The diggers were greatly outnumbered and some of the police were cruel. They stabbed the dead again and again, set fire to tents and trampled the Eureka flag into the dust.

The diggers had lost the battle. But they weren't beaten. Afterwards their complaints were looked into by the government. The licence fee was stopped and diggers were allowed to vote. The Battle of Eureka Stockade had been won.

Golden nuggets

Everyone was hard at work on the gold-field at Ballarat. Men shouted to each other, dogs barked, and blacksmiths hammered out the gold-diggers' tools. The men who worked the shafts were sweating in the heat as they heaved up buckets of dirt. Suddenly a cry went up, "Hey, lads! It's a big one!"

Other miners left their digging to race across to the group of cheering men. Twenty-two Cornishmen had found the biggest nugget the world had yet seen. This was the Welcome Nugget, and it weighed 62,850 grams. The diggers had made their fortunes with this one nugget.

All over Victoria, miners were finding huge lumps of gold. One place was called the Golden Triangle because so many nuggets were found there. And here in 1869 the biggest gold nugget of all was dug up. Heavier even than the Welcome Nugget, it weighed in at 64,750 grams! It was called the Welcome Stranger, and for gold-diggers Deason and Oates who'd found it, it was a dream come true.

Not everyone was as lucky, of course. Gold digging was a gamble – a man might dig and dig, and find nothing but dirt. His back might feel as if it was breaking as he bent over his pick under the blazing sun. His mouth would be dry, his hands blistered, and he'd often be bothered by clouds of dust or flies. But the diggers had 'gold fever' – they wouldn't give up. There was always the chance they'd find that huge golden nugget of their dreams.

The Palmer River

The small group of Chinese miners looked at the notice and slowly turned back. They'd have to return to their old spot, and rework the earth they'd already searched for gold. Carrying their picks and gold-panning tins, they retraced their steps along the creek.

By 1875 the news of the gold rush at the Palmer River had reached China. The Chinese had been using gold for more than three thousand years, and they knew how to get it from the ground. So they travelled to Cooktown in great boatloads to work in the Palmer River gold-fields.

But life was harder for the Chinese than for any other miners. Neither the white men nor the Aborigines liked them and they treated them badly. When things didn't go well for the white diggers, they picked on the Chinese. But the Chinese were patient workers, who never seemed to get tired. They could live on less and dig longer than other miners. Many worked all day up to their waists in deep water, collecting gravel from the creeks, and washing out the gold. And some of this gold reached China. It was hidden in large funeral pots full of ashes of the dead, to protect it from robbers.

Paddy Hannan accidentally discovered gold at what is now Kalgoorlie in 1893. He started Australia's richest gold rush.

The Golden Mile

The horses trotted along, carrying the three Irish gold-diggers over the rocky ground. The sun was low in the sky behind the slopes of Mount Charlotte. Then one of the horses stumbled.

"He's lost a shoe," said one of the men.

"We might as well make camp here then," said another.

And so the three men got ready to unpack their loads. A moment later, one of them fell to the ground on his knees.

"Look!" he shouted – and pointed to a glint of gold embedded in the rocks. "Look what's here!"

The Irishmen Hannan, Flanagan and Shea had started the richest gold rush Australia ever knew. The place was first called Hannan's Rush, but soon it was known by its Aboriginal name Kalgoorlie. Hannan had discovered the wealthiest two and a half square kilometres on earth – the Golden Mile. The gold wasn't only on top of the land, it went deep, deep down under the ground.

People flocked to Kalgoorlie to get rich quickly. In 1903 there were four times more people living in Western Australia than there had been ten years earlier. Hotels, bars and houses shot up and a huge water pipeline was built to connect Kalgoorlie to Mundaring Weir. Soon a whole new city had grown at Kalgoorlie. And all because Paddy Hannan's horse lost a shoe.

Russian Jack

The exhausted digger was on his hands and knees. His fingers clawed at the dry ground as he searched for water. He was desperate. Suddenly he heard a call and towards him strode a giant pushing a great wheelbarrow.

"Thirsty, friend?" shouted the huge man. "Jump aboard!" And with that he lifted the amazed gold-digger on to the barrow and started off towards the nearest well.

Many stories like this one tell of Russian Jack, the giant of the western gold-fields. Jack was over two metres tall and, like many others, he was a barrowman. These barrowmen carried all their equipment, food and water across the dry, bare country of Western Australia in search of gold. Russian Jack's barrow was a massive machine which he'd built himself. He wheeled it to the Kimberley and later to the Murchison gold finds. Along the way he'd help anyone he could.

Jack the friendly giant was also very fond of drink. Another story tells how he was found drunk by policemen, with his wheelbarrow full of dynamite. The police decided this was dangerous, so they chained Russian Jack to a great log until he sobered up. But later, when they went back to check on him, he'd gone. The worried policemen found him in a bar, the log beside him. He'd just picked it up and carried it inside!

Although life on the gold-fields was hard, it was colourful too. Characters like Russian Jack gave the diggers plenty to talk about once work had finished for the day.

The Bushrangers

The horses pulling the carriage stood up on their back legs and neighed in terror. Men and women screamed as they fell out of their seats. What was happening? The three rough-looking men called bushrangers waved pistols in the air and signalled to everyone to climb down from the coach. The passengers were shaking with fear. It was a hold-up!

The first gangs of bushrangers were escaped convicts in Tasmania who roamed about the land stealing money and precious goods from whoever they could. Travellers were robbed, inns were burgled and lonely farms were ransacked. People did what they could to protect themselves. They armed themselves with big shotguns and many ladies carried tiny pistols when they travelled. After the 1830s, nearly all these gangs were rounded up.

New bands of bushrangers grew up after the gold rush of 1851, greedy for the gold other people had worked hard for. Many bushrangers wore big hats as protection from the sun, thick shirts, tough trousers and long boots. Their clothes had to stand up to hard riding and rough living. They needed fast, powerful horses to carry them about the countryside – and away from the police. Many carried knives as well as revolvers to help them in their life of crime.

The gentleman bushranger

Martin Cash grinned at the family, slipped the money into his pocket and waved a cheerful good-bye. Then he skipped merrily out of the door with his two companions. It had been another peaceful robbery.

Cash and his friends, Jones and Kavanagh, went about on foot, robbing inns and the houses of wealthy settlers. These three were unusually polite and well-mannered, and so became known as 'gentlemen bushrangers'.

Martin Cash was an Irishman who had been transported to Sydney for seven years in 1827, for housebreaking. He worked there as a servant before leaving for Van Diemen's Land in 1837. In 1840, he was again sentenced to seven years, for stealing.

Cash led his guards a merry dance! He escaped three times in three years. While on the run, he lived the life of a bushranger and became well known as a charming and cheerful rogue.

Cash was finally captured in Hobart Town. He had killed one of the men chasing him and was sentenced to death. Instead, he was sent away for ten years to Norfolk Island, 1,400 kilometres east of New South Wales. After that, Cash quietened down. He married another Irish convict and bought a farm at Glenorchy. Martin Cash had changed from gentleman bushranger to gentleman farmer.

Ben Hall

Imagine the surprise when police turned up to arrest Ben Hall! He was a good man, a fine stockman who had done well raising cattle and horses. Here was a family man, living quietly with his wife and two young children. Here was a man who was always polite, gallant, very highly thought of in the neighbourhood. There must have been some mistake.

The people who lived in that grazing area of New South Wales couldn't believe what they'd heard. For Ben Hall was supposed to have robbed a wagon. Everyone was satisfied when the jury found him 'not guilty'.

A few months later though, Ben Hall was in trouble again. Some thought that they must have been wrong about him, but others believed that the police had a grudge against him. When Hall returned to his home at Sandy Creek he found his house ransacked and most of his stock dead. After this, Ben Hall turned bushranger. Soon he was the leader of a gang that robbed farms, stagecoaches and hotels. Ben Hall's profession had changed but he remained the same polite, peace-loving man. He forbade the use of violence against his victims.

But in the end, violence did appear on the scene. Some of the gang members were killed during robberies. And then a police sergeant was shot dead. All the romantic ideas of Ben Hall as a polite robber vanished in a puff of smoke. The gang was declared outlaw and a reward was offered for their capture, dead or alive.

Not long after this, on May 5th 1865, Ben Hall was ambushed in the swamps near Goobang Creek. He was challenged at daybreak by six police and shot dead by an Aboriginal tracker.

WANTED!

Captain Thunderbolt

Bang, Bang! Constable Walker fired at the bushranger in the river.

The year was 1870, and the bushranger who was shot in the river at Uralla was probably the man everyone called Captain Thunderbolt.

Captain Thunderbolt had become known in New England, New South Wales in the 1860s, as a robber of travellers and inns. He was an excellent horserider, and was said to treat his victims well. But the fortune he made from stealing has never been found.

WANTED!

Captain Moonlite

There was a loud knock at the door of the Union Bank. At the door stood a man with a gun.

"Let me in," he roared. "I'm Captain Moonlite!"

After he robbed the bank, Captain Moonlite was caught and put in prison. But as soon as he was set free, he gathered a gang of young men together. In November 1879 they held up Wantabadgery station near Wagga. When the police arrived, a battle broke out. One policeman and two bushrangers were killed.

Captain Moonlite was put to death in 1880.

Ned Kelly

The police had surrounded the hotel at Glenrowan. The air was filled with the sound of gunfire and bullets flew all around. Then, from out of the morning mist a bulky figure appeared, dressed in armour and a long coat. The bullets that hit him just bounced off. For a moment, the police wondered if he was some kind of spirit!

But the strange figure was Ned Kelly, a flesh-and-blood outlaw with the price of £2,000 – about $4,000 – on his head. Kelly was the leader of a gang of bushrangers and he was wanted for murder and robbery.

Kelly had first been in trouble with the police for stealing horses. He went into hiding in 1878, accused of trying to kill a police trooper. Ned was joined by his brother Dan, and the Ned Kelly gang was born.

Soon afterwards, Ned and his friends attacked four policemen who were hunting them. Three of the policemen were killed in a battle at Stringybark Creek. After that, the gang roamed north-eastern Victoria and southern New South Wales for almost two years. They robbed banks in Euroa and Jerilderie, but still they managed to dodge the police.

In June 1880 two members of the gang shot Aaron Sherritt. Sherritt had been a friend but he'd joined the police as a spy.

The Kelly gang now expected a large party of police to arrive by train. So they planned to derail the train near to the small town of Glenrowan. While they waited, the gang took

over a hotel in the town and held over sixty people as prisoners. They drank, played cards and joined Ned Kelly in a game of hop, step and jump. But the police had been warned. They arrived safely in Glenrowan, surrounded the hotel, and the shooting began. The struggle lasted all day.

Ned Kelly was able to run into the bush, but returned early in the morning to try to rescue the other three. His home-made armour didn't keep him safe for long. A policeman fired at his unprotected legs and Kelly was wounded and captured. He was the only outlaw left alive. Ned Kelly was sentenced to death for murder, and despite huge protests was hanged on November 11th 1880.

Some people saw Ned Kelly as a cruel man, but many others thought of him as a hero. He seemed to them to be standing against the unfair laws of the time. The adventures of the Kelly gang were told in stories and poems. And Ned became the most famous bushranger of all

The place for a village

In the shade of a spreading tree, a group of Aborigines had gathered. The white farmer John Batman showed them how to make their mark on the title deeds he had spread out in front of them. Each man stepped forward to 'sign' the document – with a scratchy ink mark. Now the land by the Yarra River was sold to the white settlers. The Aborigines were very pleased with the blankets, axes, mirrors, scissors, handkerchiefs and shirts which the white men had brought in payment for the land.

Until recently, John Batman had had a farm in Tasmania. He worked as hard as he could, but eventually found there was no room to increase the size of the farm.

So with some friends, he decided to look around for new land to use. They thought there must be some good farmland along the coast of Victoria, so in May 1835 they set sail.

They sailed up the Yarra River to a spot that looked promising. John Batman wrote in his diary, "This will be the place for a village." Little did he know that his 'village' would become the second largest city in Australia – Melbourne.

First however, he had to reach an agreement with the Aborigines who lived in the area, and so he persuaded them to sell the land in exchange for gifts of blankets, mirrors, tobacco and other goods. This unusual deal was not legal and Governor Bourke would not allow Batman to keep his land. But since by this time Melbourne was already established as a settlement, there was nothing he could do about it.

Melbourne became a large sprawling city, the capital of Victoria. John Batman would be amazed to see how things have changed since he grazed his sheep on the banks of the Yarra River.

The surveyor of Adelaide

Imagine being told you could just go out into a vast country and choose any spot to build a town. William Light was asked to do just that.

A number of merchants and bankers wanted to start a colony in Australia without convicts, and the British government allowed them to settle in South Australia. They appointed William Light as their surveyor-general and instructed him to look for a site to build a town. In 1836 he finally selected a place about ten kilometres inland from Holdfast Bay.

Many people disagreed with his choice. They said it was too far from the sea, and they criticized him for not surveying enough farmland nearby.

But Light made an excellent job of designing the new town of Adelaide. He planned the northern part of the city in the form of rectangles. The large central square was named after Queen Victoria and surrounding the centre of the city, with its wide streets, was a belt of pleasant parkland.

But shortly after the town of Adelaide had been established, William Light resigned as surveyor-general of South Australia. He died in Adelaide in 1839.

The wool pioneer

The British wool merchant buried his fingers in the soft fleece. "This is superb quality wool," he exclaimed. "Silky and long, it's just as good as the best Spanish wool. There'll be no shortage of buyers for Australian wool like this."

John Macarthur was delighted. It was just what he wanted to hear. The first sheep that were brought to Australia were kept for their meat, not their wool. It was only when people like John Macarthur and his wife Elizabeth started to export wool in the early 1800s that wool became important for Australia.

Macarthur was an ambitious man. He was determined to find a product which would help Australia — and himself — become rich. He was looking for something that could be produced cheaply, would not get damaged on the long sea-journey to Europe, and which would find a good market there. He thought wool was the very thing. And he was right.

Macarthur bought a few Spanish Merino sheep and started to build up a flock.

In 1801, Macarthur was involved in an illegal duel, in which his opponent was wounded. So he had to go back to England to stand trial.

The trial never took place, but Macarthur took the opportunity of showing samples of his wool to some British wool merchants. The merchants were very impressed.

Meanwhile Elizabeth had been building up the flock, and when John returned they were allowed a large grant of land. It was not long before fine wool was being exported to London. It is easy to see why Macarthur was later known as the father of the Australian wool industry.

Caroline Chisholm

The cart bumped and jolted down the dusty road. Caroline Chisholm glanced at the girls sitting on the hard benches.

Young Elsie was going into domestic service at the O'Donnell place, Jane was to work in a woollen mill outside Sydney, and Ellen was to be chambermaid in a hotel. Caroline had found the girls these jobs herself, and she was satisfied that the wages and working conditions were fair. All she had to do now was to take each girl to her new place of work. Then, she thought, each one of them would have had a fair start in her new life in Australia.

When Caroline Chisholm first settled in Sydney with her husband in 1838, she had been troubled to see the bewildering difficulties that immigrants had to face, especially the women. Many of the new arrivals had come from the big cities in Britain. When they came to Australia, they wanted to stay in the cities instead of moving to the country where there were more jobs. They found themselves living in cramped houses with very little money or food.

Caroline Chisholm didn't have much money of her own but she worked hard to raise funds from rich charities, and she got a little support from the government. She was able to open a home in Sydney for women immigrants, where the women could live while they looked around for work. Caroline thought that young settlers would be good for Australia. She thought they should set up farms in the country rather than stay in the towns. She organized meetings where new immigrants could meet each other and find out about life in Australia. In order to make it easier for people to come to Australia, she planned a way of allowing families without much money to pay for their fare after they had arrived.

Even after gold was discovered in the 1850s, people still needed the Chisholms' help. Caroline helped with travel arrangements in Britain, while her husband welcomed new arrivals in Adelaide and Melbourne.

When Caroline Chisholm became ill, she still continued to work for poor people. But in 1877, she died, after returning to Britain.

Granny Smith's apples

The Smith family had a large apple orchard at Ryde, which is now a Sydney suburb. Maria Ann Smith was in charge of the orchard while her husband Thomas was away at work.

One day in 1868, Maria Ann Smith noticed a small apple tree growing in the grass near the stream. She had no idea how it got there. It didn't look like any of her other apple trees, but it seemed to be a healthy young plant. So she dug it up and carefully moved it to a sunny place near the house, so she could keep a close watch on it.

The tree grew quickly. Very soon there were apples on it. They were unusual apples, with smooth green skins. Maria Ann Smith decided to test the apples in an apple pie. Delicious! She decided to try one of the apples raw. That was delicious too. Maria Ann Smith started to sell her new apples in the market.

The apples were so popular that she soon needed more trees. She planted seeds from the apples. In a few years, her orchard had lots of the new apple trees. She sold young trees to other fruit growers so that they could grow the new apples too. After a while, these apples became known as Granny Smith apples.

Granny Smith apples are now sold all over the world and grown in many different countries. Each and every apple is descended from that first mysterious apple tree that Maria Ann Smith found near the stream in her orchard.

Grace Bussell

The sea was rough, the surf raged and the waves pounded against the rocks. This was no time to be at sea. The steamer Georgette was in trouble. She was drifting out of control. She was being drawn on to the dangerous offshore rocks. Could the captain save the ship? The situation was desperate.

With a sickening jolt, the ship crashed against the rocks. A boy stood watching from the safety of the land and he was horrified. The ship's hull began to fill with water and she began to slip sideways. The boy raced up to the nearby Bussell farm to get help.

Meanwhile, the crew managed to let down a lifeboat and eight people began the terrifying journey to land. But the waves were too wild, the current too strong. The lifeboat overturned, throwing everyone into the sea. By the time the boy came back with Grace Bussell and Sam Isaacs, an aboriginal stockman, there was no trace of the lifeboat or the people who had been in it.

Grace and Sam were on horseback. Grace could just make out the frantic figures on the deck of the Georgette. She watched as a second lifeboat and another small boat were filled with passengers. They somehow managed to reach the shore safely. But what was to become of the other people left on the Georgette?

Without thinking of the danger, Grace urged her horse forward into the raging sea. Knocked by waves and soaked to the skin, they managed to reach the wreck. One of the passengers clasped the horse's neck and they struggled back to the shore.

Grace Bussell and Sam Isaacs plunged into the fierce sea again and again, fighting their way to the wreck. It took an exhausting four hours to rescue all the remaining passengers. Sixty-four of the seventy-two people on board were saved.

Grace Bussell was only sixteen years old that night in 1876 when she showed such amazing courage. She was given the Royal Humane Society medal two years later. Her brave act on the night of the storm made her a true Australian heroine.

Federation wheat

People stared as they passed along the road. There was that funny man again! He was dressed in a long, grey coat, huge boots and a big, brown hat. His pockets bulged with notebooks. And what was he doing? It looked as if he was tying coloured tapes to the stalks of wheat!

That's exactly what William Farrer was doing. But little did the passers-by know how important his work was. For Farrer was to become world famous as a breeder of wheat.

Farrer had travelled to New South Wales from England in 1870, with the idea of owning a sheep station. And by 1886 he owned a small, quiet station called Lambrigg, out in the bush near Canberra. Today it is part of the Australian Capital Territory.

Farrer began to experiment at Lambrigg to find some new kinds of wheat which could be grown in Australia. Wheat everywhere can suffer from many diseases, and the one that was most serious for Australian wheat at that time was called rust disease. The rust is a fungus which takes food from the wheat and makes it shrivel. Farrer set out to try to grow a wheat which could stand up to the rust. He did this by mixing different wheat plants together to make a new plant.

Many people laughed at Farrer. They thought his experiments were strange. But by 1898 he'd done so much good work that he was given a job at the town of Cowra as wheat experimentalist for the New South Wales government.

Over the years, Farrer created many new types of wheat. His most famous, called Federation, appeared in 1901. This wheat ripened early, before the rust disease could attack, and it didn't need much water, so it could be grown in dry parts of the country. It made good bread too! The new wheat was popular with the farmers straight away, and soon the fields were full of the brown-topped Federation wheat. William Farrer had created a real success.

Pioneer life

When they arrived from Europe, many settlers wanted to keep to their old lifestyle. Some people built houses like their old houses in Britain. But these weren't really suitable for the sunny Australian climate. So instead, they learned to build low houses with wide verandas. People could sleep on the cool verandas during the long hot summers.

The most common kind of early house was a slab hut. It was made of the bark of trees, built into a kind of log cabin. Ironbark trees were best because they had hard-wearing bark which was not attacked by insects.

People dressed wrongly, too. They just went on wearing what they were used to, such as thick rough woollen and flannel shirts.

When pioneers got tired of a diet of kangaroo and possum meat, they started to keep their own cows and hens, and grew their own vegetables. The land was not very good for growing crops. It needed a lot of work. And settlers also had to deal with floods, droughts, fires and pests.

Everyone on a farm worked hard. Most settlers couldn't afford to pay anyone to help with the work. But they had large families, and the children were very useful milking the cows, feeding the animals and collecting hens' eggs. A pioneer's wife hardly ever had a free minute. There was always work to be done. She had to cook, clean, make the clothes, bake bread, fetch water from the well or creek, and look after the vegetable garden, as well as helping her husband on the farm.

Nobody had very much time or energy for anything apart from work. But the settlers liked bush-dancing, sing-songs and card playing. And sometimes they organized cricket and football games, and kangaroo-chasing contests.

The pioneers set off in covered wagons, like the ones in this photograph, to find new farming land in the Australian interior.

The old post office in Timbertown.

The Sunshine Harvester

Hugh McKay's back was aching. He'd been working all day on the family farm at Drummartin in Victoria. The job that made his back ache was winnowing. It meant turning a heavy handle to blow the outside part of the wheat, called chaff, away from the grain. Seventeen-year-old Hugh thought there should be a machine to do such hard work. And so he decided to invent one!

Hugh was lucky. His father thought his idea was a good one, and his brothers offered to help. They were too poor to buy anything new, but Hugh was allowed to use whatever old machinery he could find on the farm. The boys built a workshop from logs, where the new machine could be put together.

Hugh McKay's machine was to strip the heads of the wheat from the stalks, to beat the grain from the heads and then blow the chaff from the grain – three jobs all in one! It took a lot of work before the machine was ready. But in February 1884, the family took Hugh's machine into the field to try it out. After one false start, it worked.

Hugh now needed to make more machines to sell. In 1887 he was given some money from the government, for making the best harvesting machine. He used the money to set up McKay's Harvesting Machine Company Limited in Ballarat – at the age of twenty-six.

The Sunshine Harvester was to make Hugh McKay a very rich man.

beater

grain

cutter

A stump-jump plough

Farmer Robert Bowyer Smith was hard at work ploughing his fields. His plough rattled over the earth, with a huge crash every so often whenever it met a stump in the ground. Suddenly, there was a louder noise than usual, and Smith saw that a bolt had broken. He waited for the plough to stop working – but, strangely, now it seemed to work better! Instead of the heavy crashes, it glided easily over the stumpy ground. That broken bolt was the beginning of an important invention.

Smith knew that if he could make a new plough which moved a bit like his broken one, he'd solve one of the biggest problems in South Australian farming. For at that time, ploughing over ground which was full of stumps and roots was difficult, dangerous work.

Robert Bowyer Smith was excited. Soon he got to work with his brother, Clarence, to build the first model of his new plough. The machine would ride over the stumps and then be brought back down again by heavy weights. Smith called it the 'stump-jump plough'.

In the spring of 1876 the first stump-jump plough was ready to show to other farmers. Many people laughed at the new invention – they felt that the land couldn't be ploughed properly in this way. There were also some things still wrong with the new machine, so it was not popular straightaway.

But by 1880, Clarence Smith had made a successful plough, using his brother's idea. Soon many people wanted to buy – and make

– stump-jump machines. There was talk of some money for the inventor of this wonderful new plough. Eventually in 1882 Robert Bowyer Smith was given £500, a gold medal and a plot of land by the South Australian Parliament. Robert Smith's broken bolt – and the idea it gave him – made it possible to farm huge stretches of land in South Australia, Victoria and New South Wales.

The Father of Federation

The old man with the white hair and the long, white beard stood up to make his speech. He spoke about 'a great national government of all Australia'. The man was Sir Henry Parkes and the year was 1889.

Henry Parkes had emigrated to New South Wales from England in 1839. He found work first as a labourer in the country, and later as a clerk. In 1853 he became the owner and editor of a newspaper called the Empire.

Parkes went on to become a minister of parliament. In 1872, he became premier of New South Wales for the first time – he was to be premier of the state five times. Parkes passed laws which made some important changes. He set up inspections of hospitals and brought nursing sisters trained by Florence Nightingale to Sydney. His Education Acts provided free schools for everyone.

Henry Parkes was well-known for his work towards federation. At that time, what is now Australia was six separate colonies.

Federation means the joining together of these colonies, with one government to make laws about things important to them all. It made sense to many people. Australians all spoke the same language and enjoyed the same things. By joining together, the colonies could decide who should be allowed to come to live in their country and they would be able to defend it from enemies. Together they would be stronger.

So in 1889, Sir Henry Parkes made his famous speech about federation, at Tenterfield in New South Wales. Two years later, a meeting was held in Sydney to draw up a set of rules for running the Federation. Most of the local governments raised difficulties but young Australians were keen and pressed for it. Nothing happened until there had been other meetings in 1897 and 1898.

By this time, Sir Henry Parkes had died. There had been no federation in his lifetime, but because of all his work he is often called 'the Father of Federation'.

Alone in Antarctica

Slowly, the two men made their way through the icy weather. The fierce wind whipped round their heads. The only other noise was the rattle of the dog sledge moving through the thick snow. All the time, Mawson was thinking, "We only have one day's rations left. What will we do for food?"

There was nothing else for it. The two men decided they would have to kill the dogs and eat them, one by one.

This was how explorers Douglas Mawson and Mertz spent Christmas in Antarctica in 1912. In January, Mertz died of starvation.

Now Mawson was completely alone. He was 160 kilometres from safety, in the middle of a terrible blizzard. But he kept going. The skin on one of his feet was tearing apart — so he pulled on six socks and carried on.

The weather got worse, and now Mawson was struggling to go six kilometres a day in the icy winds. Once, he staggered into a crevasse and had to pull himself out by a rope. He was getting weaker by the hour.

Luckily, Mawson came to a pile of snow called a cairn. It had been made as a marker by a search party. Inside, he found directions and some food. After eating, he set about nailing some pieces of iron to strips of wood. When he strapped them to his feet, it meant he could keep upright on the ice.

Limping along, Mawson at last reached the safety of an explorers' hut. Like a great snow-monster, he pushed open the door. For a moment he stood blinking in the light — then he stumbled through the doorway and into the arms of five surprised men. It was amazing that he was still alive.

Even after this terrible journey, Douglas Mawson went back to Antarctica to explore it by ship and by aeroplane. He was one of the world's greatest explorers, and one of Australia's greatest heroes.

128

On the beach at Gallipoli

Crack, crack! The noise of rifles and machine guns sounded across the beach. Hundreds of soldiers rushed through the bullets towards the hills. In the middle of this scramble, a little grey donkey trotted across the beach. It waited patiently while its master lifted a wounded soldier on to its back. Then it carried its passenger to safety.

It was April 1915 during World War I, and the soldiers belonged to the Australian and New Zealand Army Corps – called Anzacs for short. They were invading Gallipoli in Turkey. One of the Anzacs was John Simpson Kirkpatrick. He was an ambulance man, and his job was to find and help the wounded men.

Soon after he'd landed, Simpson saw a donkey wandering about without a driver. It was one of the donkeys used to carry water, but Simpson saw another use for this animal. It could help carry the injured soldiers.

Simpson called the donkey Duffy. Every day Simpson and Duffy would risk their lives to save others. The soldiers got used to seeing the donkey and its master moving through a shower of bullets towards a wounded man.

But one day Simpson's luck ran out. On May 19th he was shot, and Duffy came back alone.

After the war, a statue of Simpson and Duffy was put up in Melbourne, where Simpson had lived. It stands there today to remind people of the work the brave pair had done on the beach at Gallipoli.

The sky's the limit!

What a noise the two brothers made in the workshop! Hammering, banging and crashing went on day after day for nearly a year. All kinds of strange things were used – steel bands that usually held bundles of sheeps' wool together, even some wire from an old piano. But at last all the hard work was over and the secret was out. John and Reginald Duigan had built their first powered plane.

On July 16th 1910 John Duigan managed to get the plane to fly. For a few wobbly seconds it was up in the air, and it travelled for about nine metres. This was the very first flight by an Australian-built powered aeroplane.

John Duigan had set the trail for other Australian aviators to follow. In 1919, the Australian government offered a prize of £10,000 to the first Australian to fly from Britain to Australia in thirty days. Today, this journey would take just one. The Smith brothers Keith and Ross took up the challenge. Imagine how they felt as they set out from England in their Vickers Vimy plane with a distance of 18,500 kilometres in front of them. No one had ever made the journey before.

The trip wasn't an easy one. Bad weather held them up, and they had to make stops to refuel and mend damaged parts of the plane. But they made it. They landed in Australia on December 10th to the sound of claps and cheers – it had taken them just under twenty-eight days.

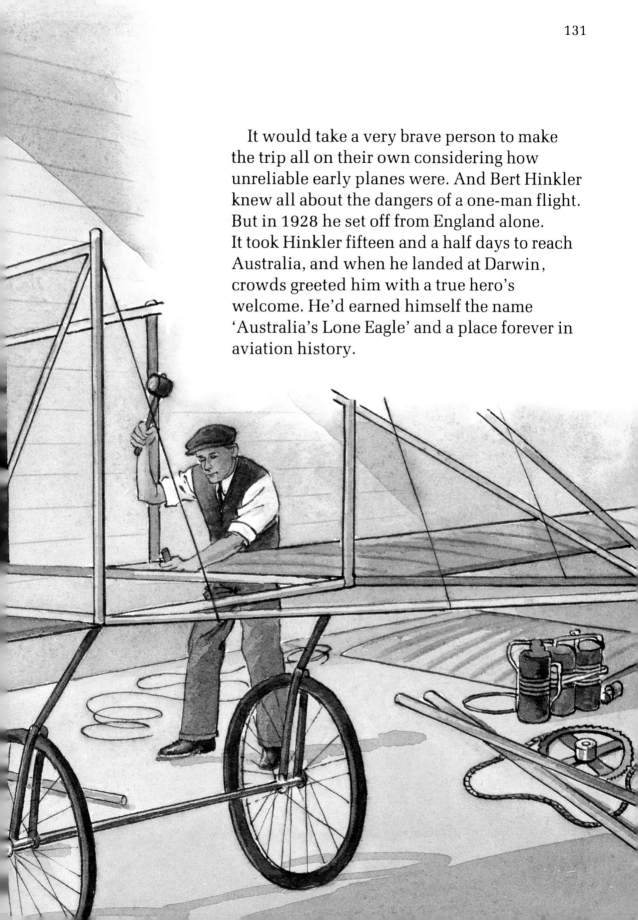

It would take a very brave person to make the trip all on their own considering how unreliable early planes were. And Bert Hinkler knew all about the dangers of a one-man flight. But in 1928 he set off from England alone. It took Hinkler fifteen and a half days to reach Australia, and when he landed at Darwin, crowds greeted him with a true hero's welcome. He'd earned himself the name 'Australia's Lone Eagle' and a place forever in aviation history.

Across the Pacific

The storm was terrible! Howling gusts of wind whipped across the open skies. The clouds were heavy and black and the little aeroplane was tossed about like a leaf. But the pilot gripped the controls and looked grimly ahead. They would survive. They had to.

In 1928, Charles Kingsford Smith made the first flight across the Pacific Ocean, from the United States of America to Australia. The conditions were terrible. He and a crew of three travelled in a three-engined aircraft called the Southern Cross. They braved furious storms and travelled over 12,210 kilometres in three days, eleven hours and eleven minutes. When they landed in Brisbane, thousands of people had gathered to welcome them. The flight made Kingsford Smith a national hero.

Kingsford Smith was trained as a pilot in the First World War. He was a brilliant beginner, and was allowed to fly on his own after only two and a half hours of lessons. After the war, he went to the United States where he became a stunt pilot. He used his skills to perform amazing flying tricks which thrilled his audiences. Stunt work added to his flying experience.

Later, Kingsford Smith joined the West Australian Airways as a pilot for the air-mail service. It was then that he decided to become the first man to fly across the Pacific.

Kingsford Smith made other exciting flights. He set a record time of twelve days and eighteen hours between Sydney and London. And on the return journey from Darwin to Britain, he set more records in solo flights. In 1934, he made the first flight across the Pacific from Australia to the United States — in a single-engined aircraft.

In 1935, Kingsford Smith made his last flight. He set off from London with another pilot, J.T. Pethybridge, hoping to make record time to Australia. But something went wrong and the aircraft disappeared somewhere near Burma. Australia's greatest pioneer of flight was never seen again.

Flying Doctor!

The little boy lay on the floor with his leg
stuck out in front of him.

"It hurts, Mum!" he groaned.

"Yes, you've broken it. But help is coming –
just lie still."

They could hear the sound of an aeroplane
overhead. Help had arrived. Soon the boy was
in the plane and on his way to have his broken
leg put in plaster. All thanks to the Royal
Flying Doctor Service.

The service was begun in 1928 in
Queensland, by the Reverend John Flynn.
He was helped by a South Australian engineer
called Alfred Traegar. Traegar had invented
the two-way pedal radio. John Flynn saw the
importance of putting radios and aeroplanes
together, to help people living in lonely places
who might be ill or hurt. In his first year, the
first flying doctor travelled over 32,000
kilometres to visit 255 patients.

Today the Flying Doctor Service works from twelve bases. If you live in a remote area and you aren't well, you can contact a doctor at your nearest base. The doctor will tell you what to do over the radio. And if you need more help, you know that a doctor can come to pick you up by aeroplane. The Flying Doctor Service helps those in pain – and sometimes saves lives.

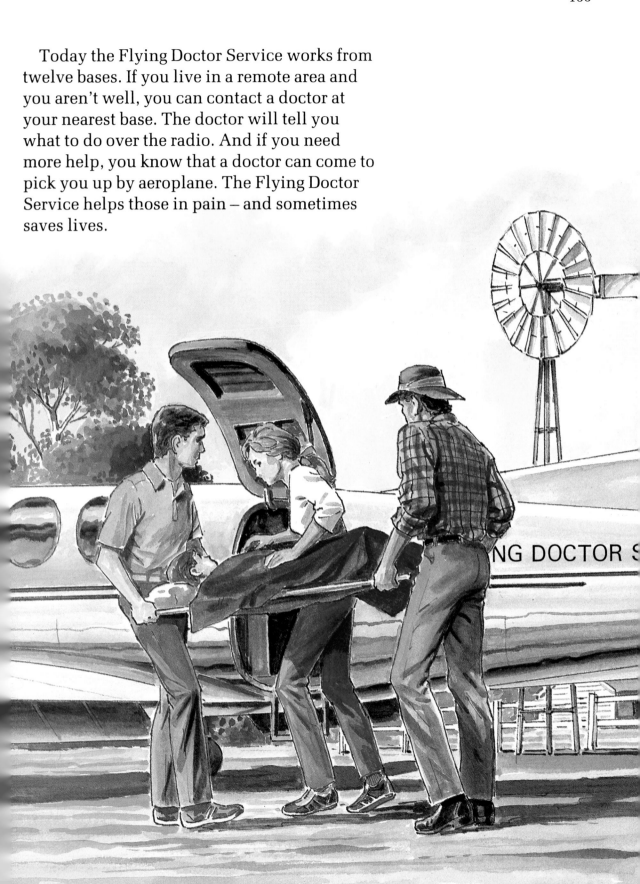

Opening the bridge

Mary and Pete shuffled from foot to foot. They didn't want to be here at all, squashed in the crowds of people. Their mother had bullied them into coming along. "It'll be a grand occasion," she said.

This was the day the great Sydney Harbour bridge was to be officially opened by Jack Lang the premier of New South Wales. 250,000 people had turned out to watch. No wonder there was a crush!

A murmur of excitement rose from the crowd. The Prime Minister, Joseph Lyons, appeared wearing a top hat and frock coat. Jack Lang followed.

The crowd cheered.

The long ribbon was stretched right across the bridge at the southern end. But Jack Lang didn't have a chance to get to the ribbon. The children watched, amazed, as a soldier on horseback galloped up at top speed, charged at the ribbon and hacked it with his sword! Then with a flourish of his weapon, he proclaimed, "In the name of the decent and respectable citizens of New South Wales, I declare this bridge open." Captain F E de Groot had beaten Jack Lang to the job.

The crowd was stunned. Mary and Pete cheered and cheered. Officials on the bridge hastily re-tied the ribbon, and Jack Lang carried on with the ceremony as it had been planned. But the children agreed that this grand occasion had turned out to be much more exciting than they'd expected.

Sydney Harbour bridge as it is seen today.

Submarines in Sydney Harbour

It was a late Sunday evening in 1942 and all was quiet in Sydney Harbour. Bright moonlight shone over the water and the night seemed peaceful. But slowly a black shape rose to the surface. Its periscope showed it to be a submarine.

Suddenly there was a terrific explosion and an old ferry-boat began to sink. At the same time, a deafening crack of machine gun bullets started up. There were enemy machines in Sydney Harbour!

People living near the harbour shot out of their beds and dressed hastily. They believed the noise was an air raid. Thousands of homes were rocked by the explosion. Pots and pans rattled on the shelves and ornaments fell to the

floor. The torpedo explosion was heard by people over a kilometre away.

Back at the harbour, the Japanese submarine was quickly pierced with bullets. Searchlights picked out the damaged vessel before it disappeared again.

In fact, three Japanese midget submarines had entered the harbour and fired two torpedoes. It was one of the few times that the violence of the Second World War came so close to Sydney.

The sports arena of the
1956 Melbourne
Olympics.

The Melbourne Olympics

Her mouth wide open and panting hard, the
girl dashed forward. Some of the crowd stood
up to watch, others leaned forward in their
seats — and all of them cheered. In an amazing
show of speed, the eighteen-year-old Sydney
girl, Betty Cuthbert, sprinted to victory in the
last leg of the 4 x 100 metres relay. It was
another win for Betty, and another gold medal
for Australia.

This was just one of the exciting
competitions at the Melbourne Olympics in
1956. The Games were opened by the Duke of
Edinburgh on November 22nd at the
Melbourne Cricket Ground. There were blue
skies and sunshine as more than 103,000
people watched athletes from sixty-eight
countries take part in the opening ceremony.

For Australia the high spot of the Games came towards the end – with the swimming. Every one of the 5,500 seats for this event had been sold months ahead. The Australian team had been on a twelve-week open-air training course at Townsville. And the training paid off. Australia won 8 gold, 4 silver and 2 bronze medals in the swimming events, to the delight of the spectators.

The Games were a success for Australia. Overall, the Australian team won a total of 35 medals – 13 gold, 8 silvers and 14 bronze medals. This is the most Australia has won at any Olympic Games. But, most important of all, Australia had planned and staged a major sporting event for countries all over the world to enjoy.

Betty Cuthbert sprinting past her rivals to win the 100 metre race.

A view of the Snowy Mountains.

The Snowy Mountains Scheme

It seems a pity that nature can't be more fair when it shares out the things it has to offer. It's too dry in Africa, too cold in the Arctic and too windy in India.

When the snow of the Snowy Mountains melted, huge amounts of water used to flow down the Snowy River towards the sea. On the way, the river burst its banks, the countryside was flooded, and a lot of damage was caused to crops and land. This happened year after year, wasting water which was badly need by the dry inland areas of Victoria and New South Wales. The puzzle for the engineers was how to stop the flooding and at the same time to channel the water where it was needed.

The result was the Snowy Mountains Scheme. There are sixteen dams blocking the Snowy River and other rivers in the mountains. And there are nearly 150 kilometres of tunnels which pipe the water into the Murray and Murrumbidgee Rivers, and send it to dry parts of New South Wales, Victoria and South Australia. On the way down the mountains, the water falls about 800 metres. This fast-moving water runs through seven power stations which generate electricity. The electricity is used in Victoria and New South Wales.

The project took 23 years to complete.

Night at the Opera

The crowd got to their feet. They shouted and clapped and stamped. The curtain rose once again. Joan Sutherland took another curtain call. The audience just wouldn't let her go. The stage was covered with 600 red roses which had been rushed all the way from Holland for the occasion.

And what an occasion it was. At last, the greatest living star of Australian opera had returned home. And she was performing in one of the most spectacular arts buildings ever made, the Sydney Opera House.

It had been expected that Joan Sutherland would be guest of honour at the opening of the Sydney Opera House. She was the obvious choice. But as it turned out, when Queen Elizabeth officially opened the building in 1973, Joan Sutherland was busy working in New York. Sydney had to wait another year before welcoming back their heroine.

The arched shells of Sydney Opera House have made it a world-famous landmark.

She did, however, sing on the building site! Nine years earlier, a cocktail party was held among the towering cranes, and Joan sang some songs from a makeshift platform.

The Sydney Opera House cost a vast amount of money to build. Much of the money needed came from holding public lotteries. The architect, Joern Utzon, planned the building in such a way that very modern engineering skills were needed to make it.

But the result is a stunning building which has become world-famous. The Opera House stands on Bennelong Point, with water on three sides. It's a building to be proud of. And musicians come from all over the world to perform in its concert halls and theatres.

Cyclone Tracy

Christmas Horror in Darwin!
Cyclone Tracy kills and injures!

On December 24th and 25th 1974, a powerful wind-storm called Cyclone Tracy brought danger and destruction to the people of Darwin.

For nearly three hours people faced a nightmare of destruction. The fierce wind rushed through the streets, tearing down walls and ripping roofs from houses. Families held on to each other to try to stop Cyclone Tracy from blowing them apart. The air was full of flying lumps of concrete, metal and glass which had once been offices and homes for Darwin people. The sound of screaming, crashing and grinding was deafening, and the rain fell in great driving sheets. Right across

the city, buildings were shattered. The new airport was completely wrecked and flooded, and ships at Darwin Harbour were driven out of control. It was as if a giant monster had crumbled Darwin in its fist.

10 pm Christmas Eve

Winds began to howl and moan and rain poured down. The force of the wind smashed windows and doors. Terrified people clung to each other as they dodged splinters of flying glass.

1 am Christmas Day

Darwin airport's wind gauge recorded a massive gust of 217 kilometres an hour. Then the gauge itself was wrecked by the wind. Radio stations failed, cutting Darwin off from the rest of the world.

3.50 am Christmas Day

Then for twenty-five minutes, a hush fell on the city. Shaken people wept with relief that they were still alive. In many parts, families crawled out from the rubble, unable to recognize their homes. But this time of quiet was not to last. It was only the eye of the storm and soon the terrific winds returned.

6 am Christmas Day

At last, Cyclone Tracy began to quieten for good. Once again, people struggled out from their hiding places. Their clothes were torn, they were bruised and injured, and their city was in ruins. Many people had been killed by the terrible storm, but many more survived to tell the tale.

A view of Canberra's first Parliament House.

A capital for Australia

An enormous pile of papers and plans covered the desk and every available space in the office. It was the closing date of the competition. Now these 137 entries would have to be sorted and judged to find the winner. It was going to be a mammoth task!

An international competition had been held to find the best design for the brand new Australian capital city, to be built on the Molonglo River. Finally, the prize-winning entry was chosen. It was submitted by an American, Walter Burley Griffin.

Twelve years earlier, in 1899, after months of discussion, an important decision had been made. The six colonies in Australia were to join together to form the federation of states. They agreed to have a central government, although they would still keep their own state government for local laws.

The central government would be housed in a capital city, the new capital city of Australia.

Where should the capital city be built? More than forty suggestions were put forward before Canberra was chosen. Then a city plan was needed. That is why the competition was held.

Since that time, Canberra has kept on growing. Walter Burley Griffin's design was so flexible that new areas of Canberra have been developed and built up without losing the feeling of spaciousness which Burley Griffin wanted the city to have.

The government is growing too. It needs more space and better buildings in which to work. In 1980, a design was chosen for a new Parliament House more than three times the size of the first one.

The new Parliament House which opened in 1988.

Sportspeople

Sir Donald Bradman is perhaps the greatest batsman cricket has known. Bradman was born at Cootamundra, New South Wales in 1908. He was captain of Australia from 1936 to 1948 and played in fifty-two test matches. Bradman's highest score was 452 not out, for New South Wales against Queensland at Sydney, in the 1929/30 season.

Sailing is one of the most popular activities in Australia. Australian yachts have made several challenges for the race called the America's Cup, which was first held in 1851. In 1983, the Australian team, headed by Alan Bond, won the race in Australia II. It was the first non-American boat ever to win the race.

Kieren Perkins began swimming after an accident at the age of nine. He earned the nickname of 'the goldfish'. By 1992 he had become the fastest swimmer in the world at 400, 800, and 1,500 metres. At the Barcelona Olympics in 1992 he won the 1,500-metre freestyle gold medal and the 400-metre freestyle silver medal.

Evonne Cawley was born Evonne Goolagong at Griffith, New South Wales in 1951. She showed special skill at tennis when she was fifteen years old. Soon she was world famous. Evonne won at Wimbledon in 1971 and again in 1980. She married Roger Cawley in 1975.

An Australian artist

The scene is a courtroom. On the left stands a judge, wearing a white wig and gown. In the middle of the picture is another figure, dressed in black. Behind, sit rows of people eager to hear what will be said. This is 'The Trial of Ned Kelly', a painting by Sidney Nolan.

Sidney Nolan was born in Melbourne in 1917. He began painting in the late 1930s and made clear, bright pictures which were full of life. He painted everything he saw around him - the busy streets, the park and the swimming baths. The Ned Kelly picture is one of a set which Nolan began in 1946. He read about the trial of the famous bushranger, went hitch-hiking to Kelly country in northern Victoria, and then began painting some of the adventures of the Kelly gang. These pictures are all painted in a bright, colourful way, just right for the lively folk hero, Kelly.

Sidney Nolan, who died in 1992, was a world-famous artist. You can see his paintings in many Australian galleries, at the Museum of Modern Art in New York and at the Tate Gallery in London.

There are many famous Australian painters, but one of the best-known is Sir Sidney Nolan.

Special words

Anzacs   The Australia and New Zealand Army Corps that fought in both World Wars.

bight   A bend or curve in the shore of a sea or river, or the water that is surrounded by that bend.

billabong   A waterhole in a river or creek that dries up during the dry season.

boomerang   An Aboriginal throwing stick used by Aborigines to hunt animals. Some boomerangs are shaped so that they curve in the air and return to the thrower.

bush   A stretch of land covered in low woody plants and shrubs.

bushrangers   Australian outlaws of the 19th century who used the bush as a hiding place.

corroboree   An Aboriginal camp ceremony with music, song and dance.

crevasse   A deep crack in a field of ice and snow.

didjeridu   A long, hollow wooden tube used as a musical instrument. A player blows through this decorated tube to make a low, ghostly wailing sound.

digger   Someone who digs for gold.

dillybag   A plaited reed basket used by Aboriginal women for carrying food that they had found.

nardoo   A paste made from the seeds of a kind of fern. It is an Aboriginal food.

station   A kind of Australian ranch.

woomera   A throwing stick with a notch in the end for inserting a spear or dart. The woomera helps sling the spear at faster speeds, and helps it go further.

Index

This index is an alphabetical list of the important words and topics in this book.

When you are looking for a special piece of information, you can look for the word in the list and it will tell you which pages to look at.

Acknowledgement

The publishers of **Childcraft** gratefully acknowledge the following artists, photographers, publishers, agencies and corporations for illustrations used in this volume. All illustrations are the exclusive property of the publishers of **Childcraft** unless names are marked with an asterisk*.

Cover	Ted Fairburn, Specs Art Agency
6/7	Mandy Doyle, B. L. Kearley Limited
8/9	Roger Jones, Specs Art Agency
10/11	Charles Front
12/13	D. Baglin, ZEFA Picture Library*
14/15	D. Baglin A.P.L., ZEFA Picture Library*
16/17	Gerald Witcomb, Specs Art Agency
18/19	Roy King, Specs Art Agency
20/21	Robert Harding Picture Library*; D. Baglin, ZEFA Picture Library*
22/23	Mandy Doyle, B. L. Kearley Limited
24/25	Tony Herbert, B. L. Kearley Limited
26/27	Roy King, Specs Art Agency
28/29	Trevor Ridley, B. L. Kearley Limited
30/31	Mandy Doyle, B. L. Kearley Limited
32/33	Gerald Witcomb, Specs Art Agency
34/35	Charles Front
36/37	The Australian Information Service, London*
38/39	Susan Hunter, Young Artists
40/41	Roy King, Specs Art Agency
42/43	Trevor Ridley, B. L. Kearley Limited
44/45	Gerald Witcomb, Specs Art Agency
46/47	Charles Front
48/49	Susan Hunter, Young Artists
50/51	Charles Front
52/53	Roy King, Specs Art Agency
54/55	Tony Herbert, B. L. Kearley Limited
56/57	Charles Front
58/61	Roy King, Specs Art Agency
62/65	Charles Front
66/67	Roy King, Specs Art Agency
68/71	Tony Herbert, B. L. Kearley Limited
72/73	Mark Peppé, B. L. Kearley Limited
74/75	Susan Hunter, Young Artists
76/77	Roy King, Specs Art Agency
78/79	Peter Geissler, Specs Art Agency
80/81	Roger Jones, Specs Art Agency
82/83	Trevor Ridley, B. L. Kearley Limited
84/85	Roy King, Specs Art Agency
86/87	Gerald Witcomb, Specs Art Agency
88/91	Ted Fairburn, Specs Art Agency
92/93	Roger Wade Walker, Specs Art Agency
94/95	Tony Herbert, B. L. Kearley Limited
96/97	Michael Strand, B. L. Kearley Limited
98/99	Susan Hunter, Young Artists
100/101	Tony Herbert, B. L. Kearley Limited
102/103	Roy King, Specs Art Agency
104/105	Mark Peppé, B. L. Kearley Limited
106/107	Duncan Harper
108/109	Michael Strand, B. L. Kearley Limited
110/111	Pat Tourret, B. L. Kearley Limited
112/114	Jo Worth, B. L. Kearley Limited
114/115	Susan Hunter, Young Artists
116/117	Tony Herbert, B. L. Kearley Limited
118/119	Commonwealth Institute Library Services*
120/121	Alan Roe, Specs Art Agency
122/125	Gerald Witcomb, Specs Art Agency
126/127	Ted Fairburn, Specs Art Agency
128/129	Susan Hunter, Young Artists
130/131	Michael Strand, B. L. Kearley Limited
132/135	Tony Herbert, B. L. Kearley Limited
136/137	Terry Thomas, Specs Art Agency; J. Allan Cash Ltd*
138/139	Duncan Harper
140/141	The Australian Information Service, London*; Roy King, Specs Art Agency
142/143	Gerald Witcomb, Specs Art Agency; Commonwealth Institute Library Services*
144/145	Tony Herbert, B. L. Kearley Limited
146/147	Roger Wade Walker, Specs Art Agency
148/149	Duncan Harper; Robert Harding Picture Library*
150/151	Michael Strand, B. L. Kearley Limited; Tony Duffy; All Sport Photographic/Simon Bruty*
152/153	Tony Herbert, B. L. Kearley Limited